T0373273

HARVARD EARLY MODERN
AND MODERN GREEK LIBRARY

Series Editors: *Panagiotis Roilos, Dimitrios Yatromanolakis*

Harvard Early Modern and Modern Greek Library makes accessible to scholars and general readers, through both original text and English translation, major works of Greek literature and thought produced in the last millennium, from vernacular Greek texts of the late eleventh century to the present.

Advisory Board

KONSTANTINOS DAPONTES

SELECTED WRITINGS

TRANSLATED WITH AN INTRODUCTION AND NOTES BY

ELINA TSALICOGLOU

HARVARD EARLY MODERN AND MODERN GREEK LIBRARY
HARVARD UNIVERSITY
DEPARTMENT OF THE CLASSICS

DISTRIBUTED BY HARVARD UNIVERSITY PRESS
CAMBRIDGE, MASSACHUSETTS
2019

Library of Congress Cataloging-in-Publication Data

Names: Dapontes, Konstantinos, 1713 or 1714-1784, author. | Tsalicoglou, Elina I., translator. | Dapontes, Konstantinos, 1713 or 1714-1784. Works. Selections. | Dapontes, Konstantinos, 1713 or 1714-1784. Works. Selections. English.

Title: Selected writings / Konstantinos Dapontes ; translated with an introduction and notes by Elina Tsalicoglou.

Other titles: Harvard Early Modern and Modern Greek Library ; 4.

Description: Cambridge, Massachusetts : Department of the Classics, Harvard University, 2019. | Series: Harvard early modern and modern Greek library ; 4 | Includes bibliographical references and index.

Identifiers: LCCN 2018020089 | ISBN 9780983532248 (alk. paper)

Subjects: LCSH: Dapontes, Konstantinos, 1713 or 1714-1784--Translations

Contents

≈

Foreword

≈

Harvard Early Modern and Modern Greek Library makes accessible to scholars and general readers, through both original text and English translation, major works of Greek literature and thought produced in the last millennium, from vernacular Greek texts of the late eleventh century to the present. Each volume offers a reliable Greek text together with an accurate and literate English translation on facing pages. The editors/translators provide wide-ranging introductions as well as explanatory notes and selective bibliographies. This new series presents current scholarship in a convenient and elegant format, aiming to make this substantial component of post-classical European literature available to researchers and students from a broad range of disciplines.

Konstantinos Dapontes was one of the most remarkable and prolific figures of eighteenth-century Greek literature. Born on the Aegean island of Skopelos in 1713, he died as a monk on Mount Athos—the most important and vibrant Orthodox Christian monastic community in the post-Byzantine world—in 1784. He traveled widely from his early youth (e.g., to Constantinople, Bucharest, and Crimea), and led an exciting and at times particularly tumultuous life: in 1746 he resorted to the court of the Khan in Crimea and the following year (1747) he was imprisoned in Constantinople for twenty months. In 1753 Konstantinos took monastic vows and was given the name Kaisarios. Occupying a rather liminal position between cultural conservatism (linked mainly with Byzantine tradition) and restrained "modernity" (inspired by the Enlightenment), in several of his works Dapontes exhibits considerable familiarity with, and an appreciation for aspects of classical antiquity and a marked encyclopedic curiosity, while remaining a steadfast supporter of the religious and ideological establishment of his time. More often than not, his writings (poetic compositions, in their majority) are interspersed with graphic autobiographical details, although not rarely his claims to the veracity and accuracy of his accounts should be taken with a grain of salt.

This volume is the first to present an anthology of representative examples of Dapontes's intriguing work to the English-speaking readership. Sections from his Geographical History, Mirror of Women, Garden of Graces, Panegyrics, and Letters on Pride and the Vanity of Human Life have been included in this bilingual edition. The translations, carefully produced by Elina Tsalicoglou, are accompanied by a detailed and enlightening introduction and notes by the translator. The publication of this book was substantially subsidized by a fund in the memory of Pia Zombanaki (1930–2007), a great admirer of Greek, especially Byzantine and post-Byzantine culture. The fund was offered by her son Andreas Zombanakis, whose generosity is here thankfully acknowledged.

Panagiotis Roilos
Dimitrios Yatromanolakis

Preface

≈

One of the most prolific writers of his age, Konstantinos Dapontes composed over twenty works, running in total to several thousand lines of verse. In selecting passages for translation from this large corpus, my aim in part has been to highlight its sheer diversity. The selections, which include complete works as well as extracts from longer ones, cover a range of genres—from hymns, letters, and auto-biography to apocryphal narratives and philosophical meditations. Most of these are written in fifteen-syllable verse, though texts penned in prose and in other metrical patterns are also represented. My aim has also been to select writings that relate to important periods and events in Dapontes's life, as well as writings that display what I felt to be a heightened poetic sensibility and which are likely to appeal to readers today.

Translating the passages turned out to be as much a balancing act as their selection. While keeping as close as possible to the original meaning, I endeavored in most cases to use the iambic pentameter in order to produce a rhythm that is as common and natural in English as the fifteen-syllable meter is in Greek, in the belief that an English-speaking reader will more easily sense the rhythmic thread that runs through Dapontes's work, even if the metrical and prosodic pattern of the original is markedly different. The translation rests on this compromise between faithfulness and flow.

All the works translated belong to the period after 1766, when Dapontes had returned to Mount Athos from his peregrinations and was devoting most of his time to the written word. As the contents of some passages relate to earlier years, I deemed it appropriate to arrange the texts not by year of composition but in biographical order, which is also the sequence in which they are discussed in the introduction. The first passage, taken from the "Geographical History," recounts the investiture of Prince Ioannes Mavrokordatos at the Sultan's palace in 1743. As one of the twenty notables invited to the ceremony, this was the closest Dapontes reached to the imperial seat of power, marking his ascent among the Phanariot elite. While this passage illustrates his eye for detail, his narrative skill is exemplified in the second text—a retelling in verse of the apocryphal story of Susanna, which he may have begun composing in his prison cell in Constantinople as early as 1747. Published much later as part of the *Mirror of Women*, a collection of stories about female figures in the Old Testament, it counts among the many of Dapontes's biblical works. The third set of extracts is taken from the *Garden of Graces*, perhaps the best known and most curious of Dapontes's works, in which he narrates the story of his life from his childhood on the island of Skopelos to the end of his *zeteia*, punctuating his account with a strange mix of digressions. The extracts here concern two periods: his three-year stay on the islet of Piperi from 1753 to 1756, where he received tonsure, changing his name to Kaisarios; and his stay on the island of Samos in 1764, where he visited the temple of Hera. The latter account gives us a rare insight into contemporary sentiments about the ancient world—not the methodical and enlightened critique of an intellectual writing from a distance, but the awe and despair of a traveler coming face to face with the ruins of his cultural past. The text that is translated in its entirety is the "Canon of Hymns Containing Many Exceptional Things," eight carefully wrought odes that capture the exuberance of the poet and his age. An earlier version of my translation was published in an anthology of Greek poetry, where I had rendered obscure and obsolete place names into accessible, modern-day equivalents.[1] I have now reversed this domesticating approach in order to preserve as much of the original text as possible, trusting that readers will find the notes sufficiently elucidating. For the same reason, I also decided to adopt the unversified layout of the original text.

Appearing on the page immediately after the "Canon of Hymns" at the end of *Panegyrics* is a short yet impassioned "Notice." This is an outspoken attack on the editors and copyists of the *Mirror of Women*, who mangled and mishandled his original work, when this came to be published in 1766. The passage affords a glimpse into some of the intricacies of book publishing in the eighteenth century; it also showcases Dapontes's prose, while hinting at his affinity with Romanticism. The present volume ends with extracts from a lesser known and more somber work, *Letters On Pride and the Vanity of Human Life*, which is suggestive of the philosophical outlook that Dapontes acquired in later life. Details of the Greek text used in the translation are given in a footnote accompanying each work.

Despite the change of his name at the time of his monastic ordination, Dapontes continued to sign his works with his lay name, "Konstantinos Dapontes," adding to it the words "renamed Kaisarios." I have used his lay name alone in the title and throughout this book to emphasize the literary continuity of his oeuvre.

≈

I would like to express my gratitude to Peter Mackridge for introducing me to Dapontes's writing during my doctoral research, sparking an enduring affection for this writer, and for also providing valuable feedback on my manuscript at a later stage; to the members of the Elizabeth Constantinides Translation Prize Committee in 2004, who perceived the value of Dapontes's verse, as well as to the editors of the Norton anthology of Greek poetry, who recognized

---

[1]   Peter Constantine et al., eds., *The Greek Poets: Homer to the Present* (New York: Norton, 2010).

the importance of making his work known to an English-speaking audience. Both strengthened my conviction that the life and writings of this lesser-known figure of the eighteenth century were worth exploring and disseminating further, eventually leading to the composition of this book. I am very grateful to the editors of the series, Panagiotis Roilos and Dimitrios Yatromanolakis, for their vision, patience, and solid support. I extend my thanks to Caroline Makropoulos for her perceptive reading of the introduction, and to Anteia Frantzi for her permission to reprint passages from *Μισμαγιά: Ἀνθολόγιο φαναριώτικης ποίησης κατὰ τὴν ἔκδοση Ζήση Δαούτη (1818)* (Athens: Ἑστία, 1993). I am indebted to David Connolly without whom this project might not have materialized in its present form. Finally, I would like to express my gratitude to my parents for being an inestimable source of support for me throughout the course of writing this book.

Introduction

〜

Worldly poet and wandering monk, Konstantinos Dapontes (1713–1784) is an enigmatic figure of the eighteenth century, who has both charmed and confounded critics from his own time to the present day. Eccentric and at the same time representative of his age, he has received considerable scholarly attention but has yet to be placed in a context that can embrace the paradoxes he presents and reveal the more profound significance of his life and work.

On the surface, Dapontes's oeuvre appears highly conventional. Drawing on the tradition of Byzantine ecclesiastical literature, it consists predominantly of religious genres: canons, scriptural exegeses, hagiographies, martyrologies, encomia, didactic dialogues, editions of liturgical and patristic texts, as well as versifications of stories from the Old and New Testament. Many of his works are also composed in fifteen-syllable verse—the traditional meter of Byzantine and folk poetry preserved in vernacular works of the Cretan Renaissance, such as *Erophile* and *Erotokritos*, which continued to be popular among Greek readers in the eighteenth century.

The conventional feel of Dapontes's oeuvre, however, belies the unconventional course of his life, which was marked by continuous moves from place to place and by prolonged periods of isolation—experiences that shaped his identity as a writer and added depth and variety to the texture of his work. A close look at his oeuvre shows that his writing, much as it was rooted in the modern culture of his age and the traditions of the past, was imbued with a subjectivity that was largely unprecedented for the literature of his time. What is more, it displays a spiritual sensibility that lends a universal appeal to his writing. With more than twenty works to his name, Dapontes was also one of the most prolific Greek writers of his age, though he hardly matched the profile of a writer in the eighteenth century: he was neither a typical enlightener—progressive teacher, merchant or intellectual championing the cause of education and freedom in line with the liberal and secular values of western Europe—nor a typical monk or cleric seeking to defend the legacy of Byzantine scholasticism and the political and religious identity of the Orthodox *millet* within the Ottoman status quo. It would not be out of place to say that Dapontes was influenced less by the dominant currents of learned culture than by the idiosyncrasies of his life and the allure of his spiritual calling.

By focusing only on his passions and peculiarities, however, one risks reducing Dapontes to a mere curiosity, an eccentric figure that had no organic relation to the wider culture of his time. Such indeed was the fate of Dapontes at the hands of several early critics, who tended to remark only on his prolific output and polymathic intellect.[2] However, Dapontes was as much a representative of his age as he was an outsider to it, for he perfectly captures in his oeuvre the change from tradition to modernity that came to define contemporary culture in the eighteenth century. The decline of Ottoman power occasioned the emergence of new social and political groups that helped spread the liberal and secular ideas of the western Enlightenment throughout southeastern Europe. As a result, the religious mentality shared for centuries by the Orthodox *millet* began to recede, giving rise to a period in which new worldviews naturally

[2]   See, for example, Papadopoulos-Vretos 1854: 194; Sathas 1868: 502–3; Sophokles 1880: θ΄–ιη΄; and Gedeon 1885: 216.

overlapped with old patterns of thought. What added to this cultural brew was a major population shift, as large numbers of rural inhabitants, crippled economically by the empire's decline, moved to the cities in search of better living conditions. Balancing on this cusp of change, Dapontes's work contains a rich and spontaneous fusion of modern and traditional culture that reflects the composite reality of the Greek world in the eighteenth century.

It was exceptionally rare for the literature of the time to embody this hybrid spirit. Contemporary writing was to a large extent the privilege of a western-oriented elite, who were more interested in bringing about a systematic revival of Hellenic high culture than in giving voice to this experience of heterogeneity. As for the clergy, a highly literate body as well, writing was chiefly a medium for maintaining the scholastic tradition of Byzantine learning, rather than depicting contemporary life at the grass roots. Furthermore, the rural base of Greek society, a considerable segment of which would have experienced these dramatic social and cultural changes, remained on the whole an anonymous and marginally literate mass that lived out a cyclical existence in accordance with the folk customs of the Orthodox Church; it asserted itself, as it had done for centuries, through the collective voice of popular traditions and religious rituals. Writing was hardly a means of expression available to them.

Born and bred on the island of Skopelos, Dapontes sprung from this rural environment. However, he was saved from silence thanks to his contact with the Phanariots who, as we shall see, placed a high premium on the written word. Even so, it is evident from his oeuvre that he did not fully adopt the writing practices of these early exponents of Enlightenment thought; nor indeed those of the clergy, despite the religious content of many of his works. Instead, he turned to the written word as a way of confessing the self, voicing the shared yet untold experience of a life caught up in the tide of change.

Unable to place him neatly in his social context, most critics until the mid-twentieth century tended to stick to the familiar facts of Dapontes's venturesome life without delving into the more complex aspects of his cultural identity. Intrigued by him though they were, given the unparalleled volume of autobiographical material he bequeathed, they perceived him as an eccentric figure, noting merely the quantity and unusual variety of his work. They rarely found any redeeming qualities in his style either: plagued by prolixity, mixed forms, and slack diction, it seemed to lack all the necessary poetic decorum, amounting on the whole to a rambling mass of unreadable verse, despite the occasional spark of humor.[3] The reappraisal of eighteenth-century Greek literature in recent decades has yielded more positive assessments of Dapontes's work, as critics have begun to take a fresh look at his writings.[4] Nonetheless, there has been no study of the essential paradoxes that lie at the heart of his oeuvre. Some scholars have touched on Dapontes's work to support their views on the question of pre-national ideologies, be this a collective Balkan mentality or a nascent national consciousness.[5] Their debate may be an all-important one, but in the case of Dapontes it is held to little avail, not only because the eighteenth century was such a monumentally transitional period in Greek culture that it inevitably embraced conflicting worldviews, but also because Dapontes himself happens to be such a heterogeneous figure that he could easily please both parties.

A Life in the Margins

Our main source for the life of Dapontes is Κῆπος χαρίτων (*Garden of Graces*), a work extending to more than 6,500 lines of fifteen-syllable

[3] For a useful overview of the negative, at best lukewarm, reception of Dapontes's work from the late nineteenth to the mid-twentieth centuries, see Kechagioglou 2009: 48n1; see also Angelou 1997: 353–62.

[4] See Vagenas 1994; Mackridge 1994; Savvidis 1995b; Angelou 1997: 17–116; Kechagioglou 2009; and Vivilakis 2013: 313–458.

[5] See, for example, Kitromilides 1996b and Mazower 2001: 62–64, on the one hand, and Vagenas 2013 on the other.

rhyming couplets, written for the most part in the vernacular form
of the language. Dapontes's overt aim in composing this work was
to give an account of his eight-year alms-collecting mission in the
Balkans and to celebrate the fragment of the True Cross believed
to have been instrumental to its success. However, the main thread
running through the work is an autobiographical narrative as
Dapontes recounts the events of his life, beginning with his child-
hood on Skopelos and ending with his stay on Mount Athos at the
age of fifty-five. Of course, as a purely historical source, the *Garden
of Graces* is not altogether reliable: its structure is hardly coherent, its
purpose ambivalent, and its content a hotchpotch of facts and fiction.
The text nevertheless remains invaluable, since no other individual in
this period recorded their life at such length. And rather than under-
mining the value of the work, its medley of myths, hymns, and other
miscellanies—much frowned upon in the past as an "unbecoming
mixture"[6]—reveals something about the possibilities of writing in
the eighteenth century, hinting too at the ways in which Dapontes's
life was intimately bound up with the written word.

Dapontes's lifelong preoccupation with writing can be traced
back to his upbringing on Skopelos and to the pivotal role that the
Monastery of Evangelistria played in his early life. No school existed
on the island, given how scant the opportunities for education were
in the early part of the eighteenth century, especially in rural areas.
But Dapontes's father, Stephanos, honorary consul of Great Britain
on the island, was so eager to see his seven children become "learned
and worthy men,"[7] that he arranged for three monks from the
Iberon Monastery on Mount Athos to come and teach the children
on the island, accommodating the school in the monastery whose

[6] "Μὴ τηρῶν . . . οὐδεμίαν εἰς τὰ συγγράμματά του τάξιν, ἀλλά συνεχῶς ἀναμιγνύων
ἀκαταλλήλως τὸ σπουδαῖον μετὰ τοῦ γελοίου, τὴν Γραφὴν μετὰ τῆς Μυθολογίας"
(Sathas 1868: 503).
[7] *Garden of Graces*, 1.37–38. Text references to the *Garden of Graces* are to chapters
and lines.

rebuilding he had helped to finance a few years earlier.[8] Despite its makeshift setup and narrow curriculum (teaching would have been confined to learning the Greek language through liturgical and other ecclesiastical texts), this school was the place where Dapontes learned to "read, write, and pray," three things which he later came to identify as "the foundations of his happiness."[9] Dapontes must have proved himself an avid learner throughout his adolescence, for his father—who, as intermediary between the Ottoman authorities and British merchants trading in the Levant, had access to influential contacts in the imperial government—soon arranged for the young Konstantinos to leave his rural homeland for the empire's more prosperous capital.

The milieu that held the promise of a career for Konstantinos and introduced him to the culture of the early Enlightenment was that of the Phanariots—the name given to the Greek elite families living in the Phanar quarter of Constantinople, near the seat of the Ecumenical Patriarchate. Well-versed in foreign languages and skilled in administrative affairs through their close ties with the head of the Orthodox *millet*, the members of these highly educated, self-styled aristocratic families were employed by the Ottoman state from the end of the seventeenth century to manage the enfeebled Porte's diplomatic relations with European powers. The few who were granted the privilege of ruling the principalities of Wallachia or Moldavia (two vassal states on the westernmost border of the empire, now comprising

---

[8] One of these monks was Hierotheos, former student of the progressive scholar and philosopher Methodios Anthrakites (1660–1736), who was brought before the Synod on charges of heresy. On Anthrakites's trial see Angelou 1988. Dapontes himself discusses the controversy in his Κατάλογος ἱστορικὸς (Historical Catalog) (in Sathas 1872: 112–13). Sources indicate that Dapontes composed a "Life of St. Hierotheos" in verse, some time between 1753 and 1758, though the text itself is missing (Angelomati-Tsounkaraki 2010). On the connection of Dapontes's ancestors to the founding of the Monastery of Evangelistria, see Patapios Kausokalyvitis 2008: 455–59.

[9] *Garden of Graces*, 5.301–6.

CR

present-day Romania) quickly came into contact with the principles and practices of the European Enlightenment. They began setting up their own printing presses, libraries, and academies of higher education in Bucharest and Jassy (the capitals of Wallachia and Moldavia, respectively), turning these cities into centers of modern learning.[10] It was in these culturally and economically vibrant cities that Dapontes, like many other aspiring Greek men of his time, would satisfy his desire for intellectual development, social mobility, and material prosperity. In the summer of 1731, assisted by his father's contacts in Constantinople, the seventeen-year-old arrived in Bucharest and followed courses in philosophy at the newly reformed princely academy, enjoying the privilege of an advanced educational curriculum taught by notable men of letters.[11]

Although he greatly welcomed this intellectual activity, Dapontes was lured by the dazzling display of wealth at the princely court: vested with exclusive rights and privileges, the Phanariot *hospodars* of Wallachia and Moldavia enjoyed a lavish lifestyle together with their families and entourage of courtiers.[12] This affluent establishment exerted such a fascination on the young Dapontes that his ambition to enter its ranks eventually eclipsed his commitment to academic study. "I passed my studies in philosophy," he writes, "but not in the right way. One cannot serve two masters at once."[13] His

[10] It was in Bucharest that Nikolaos Mavrokordatos wrote what has come to be recognized as the first Greek novel in modern times, *The Leisures of Philotheos*, in which he expresses the need for the moral betterment of contemporary Greeks. Mavrokordatos's legendary library contained an impressive range of western European works of modern philosophers, theologians, and scientists, including John Locke, Isaac Newton, and Samuel von Pufendorf; see Bouchard 1982.

[11] Dapontes studied philosophy under Georgios Chrysogonos from Trebizond, who edited Nikolaos Mavrokordatos's Περὶ τῶν καθηκόντων (1719); see *Garden of Graces*, 1.127–30, and Camariano-Cioran 1974: 381–87.

[12] For a near contemporary (though somewhat partial) account of Phanariot luxury in the principalities, see Zallony 1826: 297ff.

[13] *Garden of Graces*, 2.5–8.

desire to be admitted into the coterie of Phanariot dignitaries would have seemed to him attainable given the high-ranking contacts that his father had secured for him: the man who had taken the seventeen-year-old under his wing when the latter had initially arrived in Constantinople from Skopelos was Konstantinos Ventouras—the dragoman of the imperial fleet, governor of the Aegean *eyalet*, and a close friend of Mihai Racoviță, the hospodar of Wallachia.[14] Political stability, however, was hardly a mark of Phanariot rule in the principalities, as interfamilial rivalry, court intrigue, and popular unrest, each compounded by the fickleness of the Sultan, caused princes to be toppled from the throne, and sometimes even decapitated, as frequently and unpredictably as they were put on it. Indeed, Racoviță was suddenly removed from power three months after Dapontes's arrival in Bucharest. Deprived of immediate contacts, let alone family ties, the young islander quickly found himself a poor man and an outsider ("two great woes that surpass all others"[15]) and was left to his own devices in a society that was as ruthless as it was refined.

Disheartened though he was by the exclusion he faced, Dapontes was not deterred from pursuing his aim, relying this time on his own resources: untiring enthusiasm, a certain charm, and a knack for literary composition. Parallel to his studies, he set about working as a private tutor of Greek (the language had assumed considerable importance under Phanariot rule). He taught in the premises of the church of St. George where he was staying, as well as in the homes of local aristocratic families, which gave him ample opportunities to network within the wider community. During this time he also produced his first known works, two editions of ecclesiastical texts.[16] Dapontes worked with dogged determination, and after four years he

---

[14] Ibid. 1.67–96; Κατάλογος ἱστορικὸς (Sathas 1872: 187).

[15] "Ὅθεν καὶ ξένος καὶ πτωχὸς (δύο κακὰ μεγάλα / εἶναι καὶ ἄλλα, πλὴν αὐτά, θαρρῶ, περνοῦν τὰ ἄλλα" (*Garden of Graces*, 1.107–8).

[16] Published later, in 1736 and 1746, respectively. See the list of Dapontes's works below (pp. lxv–lxx) for details.

managed to make his presence sufficiently felt among the Phanariot potentates in the city, even to the extent of being sought as a promising match for the daughter of Konstantinos Xypolytos, chief secretary to Nikolaos Mavrokordatos, first and perhaps the most enlightened of Phanariot rulers. Indeed, soon enough he was recommended by Xypolytos to the incumbent prince of Wallachia, Konstantinos Mavrokordatos (son of Nikolaos), who hired the twenty-two-year-old as second-grade secretary (*grammatikos*) in his court.

The year was 1735 and the Russo-Turkish war had just broken out as Russia tried to gain control over the Black Sea. With the Russian occupation of Jassy, hostilities were soon to come very close to home. Dapontes was commissioned by the prince to write a chronicle of the events of this war, which he painstakingly recorded in the voluminous Δακικαὶ ἐφημερίδες (Dacian diaries) (1743).

During this time, the newly-appointed secretary was quick to win the favor of his new patron, who eventually became a keen admirer of the young chronicler's literary flair. The two men would often spend five or six hours at a time reading and composing, the prince often challenging his secretary to produce poems on unexpected themes; Dapontes always rose to the occasion and received handsome rewards in return.[17] Dapontes's spirit and skill, coupled with a fair measure of flattery and charm, not only solved his predicament of being "a poor man and an outsider," but also led him to become something of a local celebrity among the prince's literary entourage:

While I was eating, two o'clock at night,
He sent to me a servant from his home,
Who held a piece of paper in his hand—
A note on which were scribbled lines from Scripture.
He said that I was to compose on this
A single couplet, doing the best I could.

---

[17] *Garden of Graces*, 2.17–26. Dapontes included here some of these compositions (2.27–38, 45–62, 69–86, 93–110, 129–62). On his material rewards, see also ibid., 2.126, 168.

I left my meal at once and grabbed my pen
And while the boy who had come here stood around,
These verses I composed and sent them off.
Half-full, I sat back down to eat again.
The prince could hardly wait: he called for me
Forthwith and putting twenty florins in
My hand he said, "You outperform both me
And all the young and old men who are here." [18]

In the years that followed, Dapontes would rise to greater fame
and fortune but not without facing some adverse consequences.
Konstantinos Mavrokordatos failed to promote him despite
eight years of dedicated service, so Dapontes left his court and
returned to Constantinople. Here he managed to join the retinue of
Konstantinos's brother Ioannes, who had just been appointed hosp-
odar of Moldavia.[19] He was actually one of the twenty notables who
were invited to the Sultan's palace in July 1743 to attend the investi-
ture of the new prince, an event that brought him close to the imperial
seat of power for the first time, signaling his ascendancy within the
Phanariot establishment. (The passage in which he proudly recalls
his witnessing of this ceremony appears here in translation.)[20] At
Ioannes's court in Jassy, Dapontes was appointed first-grade secretary
and shortly after was promoted to the lucrative office of *caminar* (tax

[18] *Garden of Graces*, 2.115–28. On the budding literary culture of the Phanariots,
whose compositions ranged from popular moralizing verses to sentimental love
songs, see Kamarianou 1959; see also Savvidis 1991b. Manuscript anthologies of
such compositions were known as μισμαγιές. One such anthology was published in
the early nineteenth century and contained a composition by Dapontes (Daoutis
1818: 40–56; Frantzi 1993: 93–118). Selections from this composition appear here
in translation.
[19] Dapontes claims that he went to Constantinople with the intention of returning
to Skopelos and inheriting his father's office as honorary consul of Great Britain
(*Garden of Graces*, 2.243–52). This plan seems to have been abandoned as soon as
he perceived the prospect of being attached to the retinue of Prince Ioannes.
[20] "Γεωγραφικὴ ἱστορία" ("Geographical History").

collector for tobacco and alcohol). In this post he was again quick
to gain the favor of the prince, enjoying exclusive rights and rewards
along the way. In fact, within three years he had acquired such wealth
and prestige that he had become, to use his own words, "the golden
olive on the plate in the prince's court."[21]

Dapontes's sudden and conspicuous success, however, began to
breed envy. An obscure islander who had managed to rise through
the ranks, gain untold riches, and become the darling of princes, he
was perceived by other office-bearers as an upstart who had flagrantly
breached the norms of Phanariot society. Bitterness at court was exac-
erbated by his rashness: he flaunted his fortune, spoke fearlessly to
authority, and committed acts of transgression (unlawfully ordaining
a rabbi in return for a large sum of money, for instance).[22] The contro-
versy he courted soon reached Constantinople and in the summer
of 1746 an order arrived calling for his arrest.[23] Dapontes's lack of
family ties at this point proved fateful. No literary talent or princes'
favor could extricate him from the web of Phanariot intrigue, and
his career in the principalities dissolved into "dust and smoke."[24] It is
quite ironic that the social handicap which earlier had acted as a spur
to his success was now the very factor that precipitated his downfall.

Unable to countermand the order for his arrest yet reluctant to
deliver him into enemy hands, the prince arranged for Dapontes to be
furtively dispatched to Crimea on the northern coast of the Black Sea
and to be granted asylum in the palace of the Khan in the capital city

[21] *Garden of Graces*, 3.137–38, 201–11.
[22] Ibid. 3.153–56, 187–200, 301–54.
[23] The mandate was most likely issued by Ioannes's *kapikahaya* (the prince's offi-
cial representative in the Sublime Porte), whose son Antonakes Radamanes was
postelnic (foreign affairs officer) at the prince's court in Jassy and Dapontes's arch-
enemy. Radamanes had contrived on several occasions to have Dapontes ostracized.
For a comprehensive account of this embroilment, see Paizi-Apostolopoulou 2007a:
120–31.
[24] *Garden of Graces*, 3.369–70.

of Bakhchisaray. This destination was a safe one since Crimea maintained good relations with Moldavia as joint ally against Russia, and, being a vassal state, was generally free from Ottoman interference.

Flung to a remote corner of the Empire and far removed from the life and lands he knew, Dapontes found himself an outcast once again. Yet this time, exclusion, rather than intensifying his ambition, paved the way for a spiritual awakening.[25] Spending most of his time hunting in the forests or rambling along the rivers, either on his own or in the company of a French doctor who also happened to be residing in the palace at the time, Dapontes was filled with joy by the simplicity and the serenity of his physical surroundings, and his former desire for worldly prosperity began to pale in comparison.[26] What triggered his awakening was a visit to the fifteenth-century Uspensky cave monastery, carved out of the towering rock face on the outskirts of Bakhchisaray. He gasped in astonishment as he thought of the hermits who once resided in the caves, admiring the strength of their faith; they seemed to him "as though they were hanging between heaven and earth like Christ on the cross."[27] The awe he felt, foreshadowed no doubt by the love for prayer he had felt as a child in his father's monastery, was so great that for years to come the memory of this visit moved him to tears.[28] More significantly, it led him toward a radical reassessment of his former conduct, paving the way for his own life of ascetic prayer.

[25] Dapontes's experiences in Crimea are not recounted in the *Garden of Graces* but in the second volume of Καθρέπτης γυναικῶν (*Mirror of Women*, 2: 289–322, 400–406). Text references to the *Mirror of Women* are to volumes and pages.

[26] He refers to his exile as a "blissful wandering" ("Μίαν δὲ περιήγησιν, καὶ τόσον μακαρίαν") that he could never have experienced in Moldavia. "So many men will rise to Caminar," he writes, "but very few are honored with this exile" (*Mirror of Women*, 2:306).

[27] Ibid., 2:303.

[28] Ibid., 2:302.

This spiritual awakening was to take a more drastic turn following another, rather unexpected experience of isolation. Lulled into a false sense of security after eight months of peaceful exile, he made the mistake of accompanying the Khan on an official visit to Constantinople, where the news of his residence in the city's cosmopolitan quarter of Pera reached his ever-vigilant enemies. In the early hours of a spring morning in 1747, not long after his arrival, he was arrested in his bed and thrown into prison.[29] According to his "Ἐγκώμιον φυλακῆς" (Encomium of Prison Life), Dapontes welcomed this twenty-month confinement as an exercise in ascetic discipline. He claimed that imprisonment taught him the virtues of humility and contrition, while giving him the opportunity to atone for the sinful existence he believed he had led in Moldavia and Wallachia.[30] As with other writers in other times (Oscar Wilde, for instance), his imprisonment not only deepened his faith but also set him writing: he began working on what was to become one of his main literary works, *Καθρέπτης γυναικῶν* (*Mirror of Women*), a two-volume collection of edifying stories about women from the Old Testament, rendered into fifteen-syllable verse.[31]

This time Dapontes was not writing for the pleasure of princes or even simply for the moral improvement of his readers. He was searching for his own voice: he inserted private musings and autobiographical

[29] Ibid., 2:307–8.
[30] The "Ἐγκώμιον φυλακῆς" appeared in Dapontes's *Πατερικὸν τοῦ ἐν ἁγίοις πατρὸς ἡμῶν Γρηγορίου τοῦ Διαλόγου πάπα Ῥώμης . . .* (Paterikon, 1780), pp. 544–76. Further remarks in praise of his experiences in prison appear in the *Garden of Graces*, 4.87–96, and in a letter to Bishop Dionysos of Skopelos: "My imprisonment was necessary; it was essential. . . . It was a bitter and painful experience, but it became my salvation and that is why I have written an encomium in its praise" (Legrand 1880–88, 1:τοε΄). Dapontes wrote several letters during his incarceration. These can be found in Karanasios 2016: 293–305, 323–38. For a detailed discussion of the historical circumstances surrounding Dapontes' imprisonment see Karanasios 2016: 276–93.
[31] On the dating of the *Mirror of Women*, see Kaplanis 2001: 57–59. Dapontes probably completed the work in 1756; it was not published, however, until 1766.

digressions, and experimented with a distinctly dramatic style.[32] As an example of this development, one can cite his version of the Old Testament story of Susanna.[33] Dapontes transforms this short apocryphal story into an extended narrative, enriched with descriptive detail, characterization, imagery, and other stylistic devices. For instance, the depraved elders that attempt to seduce Susanna are compared to "black crows around a white dove" or to "rabid dogs" that "gnash their teeth" as they feast their eyes on the beautiful woman. While in the original story the assembly that listens to the elders' false charges and to Susanna's death sentence is little more than a gathering of mute and passive spectators, in Dapontes's version it springs to life: they "tear their cheeks" and "stand in shock with trembling hands"; the locals "shut their shops and leave their work behind to join in the cries and lamentations." Dapontes sees opportunity for dramatic tension in places where the original narrative states a fact plainly and simply—as at the end, where the elders are found guilty and sentenced to death. Here Dapontes imagines a vigorous and fiery crowd that ardently participates in the condemnation: some hurl "soil and sticks" at the wicked elders while others, less equipped but just as keen, remove their shoes and pound them down, cursing all along. Interestingly, Dapontes presents the entire story in the form of a dialogue between two fictional characters, Psyche and Chariton, the latter imagined as a witness of the events who narrates these to Psyche while responding to her questions and reactions. Perhaps the most evocative part of Dapontes's version is the description of Susanna's sensuous stroll in her husband's fragrant and bird-filled garden—a digression that one cannot but link to Dapontes's

---

[32] On the dramatic style of the *Mirror of Women*, see Vivilakis 2013: 311–458.

[33] Dapontes was not alone in rewriting this famous biblical story, and he may have even been familiar with the sixteenth-century version written by Patriarch Meletios Pegas (Vivilakis 2013: 136–43). One wonders whether he would have also been familiar with the western literary tradition of this story (Clanton 2006). Dapontes returned to the story of Susanna, in dialogue form, in his "Φανάρι γυναικῶν" (Lantern of Women).

own delight in the plants and pleasures of gardens, as will be discussed below. It is striking how a stirring and spirited narrative as this could have been conceived, if not also composed, in the bleak conditions of prison life.

In the five years that followed his release from prison, Dapontes attempted to resume a life of normality. He resided for a few months on the island of Halki in the company of several religious dignitaries, many of whom he had befriended during his time in the principalities. They urged him to marry, and in November 1749 Dapontes eventually acted on their advice, marrying the daughter of a well-to-do family from Constantinople.[34] This marriage, however, lasted no more than two years, for shortly after childbirth both his wife Mariora and his daughter passed away.[35] Stricken with grief and divested of all his wealth, Dapontes soon came to the decision to take monastic vows. He might have considered the monastic life as the obvious answer to his financial and emotional distress, the latter compounded by the intense remorse he felt after refusing, out of shame, to see his aged mother who had expressly traveled from Skopelos to visit her son in prison and who had died three months later—an event movingly described in his autobiography.[36] However, his decision to become a monk (hardly an unusual path for men to follow at the time) was not prompted by these concerns alone. Dapontes was genuinely disillusioned with the desires of worldly success and was eager to seek a life of solitude:

[34] *Garden of Graces*, 4.97–126. Because of his imprisonment, his earlier engagement to Xypolytos's daughter had been broken. See Karanasios 2016: 283.

[35] In the *Garden of Graces* Dapontes passes over the years of his marriage, a hiatus which could suggest an emotional detachment. However, a manuscript containing poems that Dapontes wrote during his engagement with Mariora reveals the depth of his feelings. See Kechagioglou 1986: 50–54.

[36] *Garden of Graces*, 4.63–86. Dapontes's compassionate nature and affection for his mother are also evident in a letter that he wrote to her from Bucharest when his younger brother passed away (Legrand 1880–88, 1:τνς΄–τνη΄).

Perceiving then how futile this world was
And having had my fill of things both good and bad,
My worldly ways I came to loathe and leave,
And sought to live a life of solitude.
(*Garden of Graces*, 5.1–10)

So it was in the late summer of 1753 that he set sail from Constantinople and reached Piperi, a small island situated northeast of his home island of Skopelos. Encircled by rocky cliffs and a precipitous coastline, it was on this desert islet, dotted only by a couple of churches and a small monastery, that Dapontes received tonsure, changing his name to Kaisarios. Yet even in this forsaken speck of land in the midst of the Aegean, peopled only by a brotherhood of ten monks, Dapontes managed to turn himself into an outsider once again. For reasons he avoids giving, he was repeatedly cast out by the abbot "like a black sheep," allowed to join the other monks only for meals and Sunday worship. However, this new period of exclusion paved the way for what was, on his account, the most spiritually uplifting period of his life. He spent most of his time in the garden near his cell, planting and gathering fruit and vegetables—an activity that led him to perceive the goods of the earth as gifts from God to be savored to the fullest. In his eyes, he was living in a "paradise of pleasures." He enjoyed perfect health too, as the painful bouts of gout that he used to suffer from disappeared.[37] Enveloped in this feeling of bliss, Dapontes not only confirmed his forgoing of past indulgences ("wealth, women, and courtly banquets"); he also experienced a profound sense of gratitude,[38] close perhaps to the eucharistic reci-

---

[37] *Garden of Graces*, 5.259–60. His gout came back in later life (ibid., 9.106–10).

[38] The passage entitled "Ἐγκώμιον ἐρημίας καὶ μοναχικῆς διαγωγῆς" ("In Praise of Solitude and the Monastic Life") (ibid., 5.107ff.), which appears here in translation, is infused with this sense of gratitude. Some readers consider this passage to be one of Dapontes's finest pieces of writing: "[It is] the best thing of his I have ever read. Daponte [sic] wrote thousands and thousands of lines, but here alone do I catch the sound of a real experience set down with genuine sincerity" (Dawkins 1936: 68).

procity between God and man lying at the heart of the Orthodox faith, and one that he would attempt to reproduce years later in some of his hymns. From his account it appears that he also practiced a form of unceasing inner prayer, similar to the hesychast tradition of silent contemplation—a comparison we shall return to later.[39] Deeply moved by joy, he became highly creative as well, for when he was not in the garden working, he was in his cell writing. He claims to have composed on Piperi more than ten volumes of verse.[40] It is not surprising that Dapontes recalls the three years he lived on the island as the happiest period of his life, the metaphor for his small garden serving appropriately as the title for his autobiography as a whole.

Dapontes's euphoria was cut short following a decisive clash with the abbot, who permanently dismissed the forty-three year old monk from Piperi in November 1756. Dapontes had no choice but to go to his homeland, less than a day's sail away. He stayed on Skopelos for the next few months before setting off again, this time to Mount Athos, with a view to staying on the Holy Mountain for an extended period. He resided at the Xeropotamou Monastery, possibly because of his acquaintaince with the *skeuophylax* (the custodian of the monastery's sacred utensils), who was also from Skopelos. But hardly three weeks after his arrival, he was urged by the brotherhood to go back to Wallachia to secure financial support for the rebuilding of the *katholikon* (the main church of the monastery), which had recently been damaged by fire. Their request was not unusual, for alms-collecting missions of this kind (known as *zeteiai*) were common at the time, with Phanariot princes regularly serving as generous benefactors.[41]

---

[39] *Garden of Graces*, 5.44–45, 143–218.

[40] *Garden of Graces*, 5.39–41. It is not clear whether these were published later or whether they remained in manuscript form and have been subsequently lost. When he made this claim in 1768, only four works are known to have been written: Λόγος . . . περὶ ἐξόδου ψυχῆς (On the Departure of the Soul) and *Mirror of Women*, published in 1763 and 1766, respectively; and the unpublished "Φανάρι γυναικῶν" and "Ἄνθη νοητά," composed in 1764 and 1768, respectively.

[41] See Angelomati-Tsounkaraki 2007: 260, 265.

The brotherhood knew of the prestige that their visitor used to enjoy in the Phanariot courts. Dapontes was initially reluctant to return to the principalities for fear of falling back into a life of sin, but he eventually agreed to their request after he was permitted to take on the journey a fragment of the True Cross, the monastery's most treasured relic, "as a guardian of [his] soul."[42]

With the relic close at hand and accompanied by two other monks, Dapontes set sail from Mount Athos on 21 May 1757. Their initial plan was to go directly to Constantinople and the Danubian principalities but their mission soon took the form of an extended peripatetic journey to hundreds of villages, towns, and cities throughout the Balkans. The party first sailed past the coast of Thrace and then trekked northwards into the Bulgarian and Romanian heartlands before journeying southeast toward Constantinople. Following an extended stay in the Ottoman capital, where Dapontes's contacts among wealthy Phanariots proved indispensable for the success of the mission,[43] they sailed to several Aegean islands, including Chios, Samos, Psara, Skopelos, and Euboea. They returned to the Holy Mountain on 11 September 1765, having collected an impressively large number of donations.[44]

Their itinerary and choice of stopovers were determined as much by what has been termed a "geography of faith"[45]—the network of places possessing a common heritage of Orthodox culture (and hence a shared belief in the miraculous power of the True Cross), supplying the traveling monks with shelter and sustenance—as by the proximity of places to trade routes with western Europe, for the inhabitants of commercially active cities were more likely to be lavish in their support of the monks' charitable cause. The party thus spent several days in places where lodging was provided by monasteries,

[42] *Garden of Graces*, 5.354.
[43] See Polyviou 1992: 195–200.
[44] For a full description of the itinerary, supplemented with details of the various alms collected during the mission, see Polyviou 1992: 194–98; 1999: 37–47.
[45] Kitromilides 1996b: 178.

such as Xeropotamou's monastic dependency in the coastal town of
Aenus (modern-day Enez) on the southeastern coast of Thrace and
the seventeenth-century monastery in the Romanian city of Galați
on the banks of the Danube. Similarly, they stopped at places known
for their commercial vitality, such as Adrianople (modern-day
Edirne), the prominent city of Veliko Tarnovo in central Bulgaria,
the resource-rich trading city of Focșani near the border between
Wallachia and Moldavia, and Chios, whose manufacture of silk and
mastic gum had made it one of the wealthiest islands in the Aegean.[46]
Dapontes's eight-year-long peregrination around the Balkans
heightened the sense of displacement that he had endured on many
occasions in the past and that had become by now a familiar part
of his life: he had been an outsider in the principalities, an exile in
Crimea, a prisoner in Constantinople, and a pariah on Piperi. Living
as a wandering monk for almost a decade only intensified this feeling:

I grew tired of traveling around the world
And walking through each country, short of rest.
I roamed from place to place for years and years
And never settled down or found repose.[47]

Too weary and preoccupied with the practicalities of the mission,
Dapontes produced little writing during his travels. He published
only a translation of a theological treatise by St. Cyril of Alexandria,
Λόγος . . . περὶ ἐξόδου ψυχῆς (1763), and composed the unpublished
"Φανάρι γυναικῶν" (1764). However, when he was back in the soli-
tude of his cell, he resumed his literary activity with a vengeance. He

---

[46] The party planned to travel also to Smyrna, an equally prosperous city. However,
the outbreak of a grape disease on the nearby island of Samos, where the inhabitants
pleaded to have the relic's blessing, forced them to change their itinerary (*Garden of
Graces*, 10.51–64).
[47] "Διότι ἐβαρέθηκα τὸν κόσμον νὰ γυρίζω, / τὲς χῶρες νὰ περιπατῶ, στάσιν νὰ μὴ
γνωρίζω· / τόπον ἐκ τόπου πάντοτε τόσον καιρὸ ν᾽ ἀλλάζω, / εἰς ἕνα τόπον καὶ ἐγὼ
νὰ μὴν ἐφησυχάζω" (*Garden of Graces*, 12.1–4). For a vivid account of Dapontes's
frenetic tour around the different neighborhoods of Constantinople, see ibid.,
9.1–104.

saw to the publication of the *Mirror of Women*, which embroiled him in a bitter dispute with the editor (the "Notice" expressing his grievance appears here in translation), and within three years he composed two works that amounted to more than 16,000 verses: "Ἄνθη νοητά" (Flowers of thought), a collection of biblical stories and miscellaneous items relating to contemporary Orthodox culture; and the *Garden of Graces*, which contained a great deal more than an account of the mission stated in the full title of the work.[48] Considering that he was heavily involved in planning and overseeing the restoration of the *katholikon* at the same time, Dapontes's literary output in this period is even more impressive.[49]

Despite the evident weariness that Dapontes had felt in the course of his travels, these writings—as well as others that followed—convey a strong sense of exuberance, especially with regard to place. Geographical catalogs and comparisons abound: "Ἄνθη νοητά," for example, contains an extensive list of Orthodox monuments located in Asia, Africa, and the Balkans;[50] and the "Κανὼν περιεκτικὸς πολλῶν ἐξαιρέτων πραγμάτων" ("Canon of Hymns Containing Many Exceptional Things"), which is discussed below, makes reference to an astounding number of place names, ranging from western Europe, the Balkans, and Russia to the African continent, the Middle East, and the Far East. In one of his last works, the unpublished "Γεωγραφικὴ ἱστορία" ("Geographical History," 1781–82), in which he takes a more systematic approach to the subject, Dapontes's interest in place reaches its apogee.

[48] The full title is: Κῆπος χαρίτων· τουτέστι, βιβλίον περιέχον τὴν περίοδον τοῦ τιμίου ξύλου τοῦ ζωοποιοῦ σταυροῦ, τοῦ ἐν τῇ ἱερᾷ καὶ βασιλικῇ Μονῇ τοῦ Ξηροποτάμου, τῇ οὔσῃ ἐν τῷ ἁγιωνύμῳ Ὄρει τοῦ Ἄθωνος, καὶ ἄλλα διάφορα....

[49] For details of Dapontes's involvement in the restoration of the *katholikon*, an activity less known compared to his literary achievements, see Polyviou 1999: 48–87. Dapontes was also involved in the selection of the church's iconography, which consisted of an unusually large number of neo-martyrs (Polyviou 1996; Paschalides 2012).

[50] Papadop[o]ulos-Kerameus 1909: 279–311.

Various factors contributed to Dapontes's fascination with place:
the increased production of maps commissioned by large monas-
teries and donated to benefactors by missionary monks;[51] the
Enlightenment interest in geography as a field of scientific inquiry;[52]
the popularity of traveling and travel-writing as a source of secular
knowledge in both Greek and Ottoman culture[53]—all of these
combined to stimulate his imagination, provide him with source
material, and heighten his sense of wonder. His spiritual sensibility
would have played an important part too, for in the same way that
he regarded the goods of the earth as divine gifts to humankind,
Dapontes saw "the kingdoms, cities, and sheer expanse of the earth"
as a sign of God's grace and a reason for worship.[54]

On a more personal level, the reason for his joy seems to be that
traveling—and, more importantly, writing about his travels—gave
him a new sense of belonging. Years spent far from his homeland had
eroded his sense of rootedness. But now, brimming with impressions,
inspired by the geographical imagination of his age, and filled with a
holistic view of creation, he saw himself as an ecumenical inhabitant
who had the world, quite literally, at his fingertips. In the *Garden of
Graces* he mentions how reading and writing about a place can trans-
form one into a "native" inhabitant of that place.[55] His claims to have

---

[51] Tolias 2010: 12.

[52] Koumarianou 1988: 9–79. Patrick Gordon's influential three-volume *Geography
Anatomiz'd; or, the Geographical Grammar* was translated by the enlightener Georgios
Fatseas as Γραμματικὴ γεωγραφική, which appeared in 1760, only a few years before
Dapontes composed the *Garden of Graces*.

[53] Minaoglou 2007. Dapontes's contemporary Vasileios Vatatzis (1694–1748) is
an interesting case in point. A merchant from Constantinople, he wrote extensively
(in verse) about his travels in Europe and Asia, adding several maps to his work
(Angelomati-Tsounkaraki 2000: 175–78). His writings remain unpublished.

[54] "... ἡ γεωγραφίαις / ... τοῦ θεοῦ τὴν δόξαν διηγοῦνται / ὡς καθὼς καὶ οἱ οὐρανοὶ
τοὺς οὐρανοὺς μιμοῦνται· / διότι γράφοντες ἡμεῖς τῆς γῆς τὰς βασιλείας / τῆς γῆς τὰς
πόλεις, τὰ καλά, καὶ τὰς εὐρυχωρίας· / δοξάζεται ὁ Κύριος κατὰ ἀκολουθίαν / ὁποῦ τὰ
ἔδωκεν αὐτὰ διὰ φιλανθρωπίαν" ("Geographical History," in Legrand 1881: 252–53).

[55] *Garden of Graces*, 10.65–74.

traveled to "many countries in Europe and Asia," countries that he never actually visited, further indicate the vicariousness with which he related to place, revealing how eager he was to perceive himself as a global traveler.[56] If writing helped him to give shape to an identity that was kept in flux by a life of continual upheaval, writing itself may be regarded as the only "place" to which he truly belonged.

Even in the last two decades of his life, despite being less mobile as the years went by, Dapontes never settled down in a single place: he switched twice between the monasteries of Xeropotamou and Koutloumousiou, then left Mount Athos altogether and stayed on Skopelos for six years,[57] only to return again to Xeropotamou Monastery in the summer of 1784, a few months before his death. The single constant amid this restless movement was his writing: he continued composing until the very end of his life, averaging one work every eighteen months. This unwavering enthusiasm is illustrated aptly in a passing remark entered in his private notebook:

> In the same year [1772], on the feast day of Saint Demetrios following the vespers for Saint Nestor, Friday it was, while I was writing my "Book of Kings," I composed eighty-two verses using only one filling of ink, without dipping my quill in a second time. God, who is all-knowing, knows that I am not lying. It was an extraordinary thing indeed, and one that had never happened to me since the

---

[56] Ibid., 11.1–2.

[57] Details of Dapontes's activity on the island during this period, as well as a transcription of the log he kept recording various events and transactions, especially those relating to the monastery of Evangelistria, can be found in Kallianos 1987.

age of seven, when I held a quill for the first time
as a child and began to write. I have been writing
ceaselessly ever since until this day—and I am now
fifty-nine years old.[58]

The only existing portrait of Dapontes, which shows him lost in
thought at the side of a small desk with his left hand poised on the
blank page of a journal and his right hand holding the *kondyli* (a type
of quill pen) in a state of readiness, captures the passion of his youth
that was to stay with him until the approach of old age. He died on
Mount Athos on December 4, 1784, at the age of seventy-one.

Eccentric or Representative?

Despite being one of the most prolific writers of his age, Dapontes
hardly matched the typical profile of a learned Greek in the eigh-
teenth century. Most educated young men of the time usually pursued
advanced studies in western Europe, where they joined the diaspora
network of teachers, publishers, merchants, and scholars committed
to the cause of cultural progress. Dapontes never went, or ever enter-
tained the idea of going to western Europe. Between 1753 and 1759
many educated young men also flocked to the Holy Mountain to
attend lectures at the Athonite Academy, which had become famous
for its modern curriculum and progressive teaching methods under
the directorship of the illustrious deacon and scholar Eugenios
Voulgaris.[59] Dapontes arrived on Mount Athos precisely when the
Academy was at its peak, but it appears that he never actually visited it

---

[58] "Τῷ αὐτῷ ἔτει, ἀνήμερα τοῦ ἁγίου Δημητρίου, μετὰ τὸν ἑσπερινὸν τοῦ ἁγίου
Νέστορος, ἡμέρα Παρασκευή, γράφωντας τὸ βιβλίον μου τῶν Βασιλειῶν, ἔγραψα μὲ
μίαν κονδυλιὰ μελάνης, δίχως νὰ βουτήσω δεύτερον, στίχους ὀγδοῆντα δύο, οἶδεν ὁ
Θεὸς ὁ τὰ πάντα εἰδώς, ὅτι οὐ ψεύδομαι. Πολὺ τῇ ἀληθείᾳ πρᾶγμα ναὶ καὶ ἐξαίσιον καὶ
ὁποῦ ποτὲ ἄλλοτε τοιοῦτον τί εἰς ἐμένα δὲν ἔγινεν, ὁποῦ ἀπὸ ἑπτὰ ἐτῶν σχεδὸν παιδίον
ἔπιασα τὸ κονδύλιον καὶ ἄρχισα νὰ γράφω, καὶ γράφω σχεδὸν ἀδιακόπως ἕως τῆς
σήμερον πενῆντα ἐννέα χρονῶν ὁποῦ εἶμαι" (Kadas 1988: 198).
[59] On the Academy, its establishment, curriculum, and history, see Kitromilides

and makes only a passing reference to it in his work.[60] In fact, despite being acutely aware of the cultural backwardness of his *genos*,[61] and of the need for moral betterment, Dapontes hardly ever took part in the intellectual discourses practiced by his peers: he maintained little scholarly interest in philosophy or science,[62] produced no translations of secular western literature, and never dealt systematically with the issue of language. Even as a monk, Dapontes was unlike those contemporaries (Daniil Philippidis, Veniamin Lesvios, or Kosmas Aitolos, for example) who combined their monastic calling with a commitment to the broader Enlightenment cause. It comes as no surprise that he never rates a mention on the usual roll call of the Greek intelligentsia of the eighteenth century.[63]

Not a mainstream figure, Dapontes happens nonetheless to capture in his oeuvre the spirit of his age, a time of gradual cultural change during which the liberal, secular ideas of the Enlightenment overlapped with those of traditional religious thought. On numerous occasions his writing contains a rich and spontaneous fusion of these

---

1996a. Among its students were Iosepos Moisiodax and Christodoulos Pamblekis, who were to become key figures of the Greek Enlightenment.

[60] "Περὶ τοῦ σχολείου τοῦ Ἁγίου Ὄρους" ("Concerning the Academy on the Holy Mountain"), in "Ἄνθη νοητά" (Veis 1942: 19). The reason why Dapontes did not attend the Academy might have been purely practical: his first visit to Mount Athos was brief, and the Academy, annexed to the Vatopedi Monastery on the other side of the peninsula, was at a considerable distance from the Xeropotamou Monastery, where he was staying. On the other hand, he does mention that during the short time of his first visit he had the opportunity "to visit five or six other monasteries" (*Garden of Graces*, 5.317–18); it is likely that Vatopedi was one of them (ibid., 10.98).

[61] Ibid., 11.35–58.

[62] He is entirely frank about his half-heartedness toward the study of philosophy (*Garden of Graces*, 2.5–8). Dapontes's non-involvement in the Hellenizing activities of his contemporaries is discussed further in Costache 2010/11: 44–45

[63] See, for example, the appendix in Mackridge 1981. On the popular evangelist and missionary Kosmas Aitolos, who was a student of Voulgaris and is said to have set up hundreds of local schools in Thessaly, Epirus, and Albania, see Cavarnos 1985; Kitromilides 1996a: 267–68.

two worlds of thought, placing him at the heart of his culture rather than in its margins. This is well exemplified in his reaction to the ruins of the sixth-century temple of Hera on Samos (the passage appears here in translation),[64] a response that combines the historical awareness that was growing among enlighteners, with the popular sentiment of traditional culture. On the one hand, he shows an awareness of and restrained respect for the Greeks' ancient lineage, deploring the ignorance, idolatry, and prejudices of his generation—all thoughts typical of Enlightenment criticism. On the other hand, he directly attributes the intellectual achievements of the ancients and the cultural inferiority of his age to a divine agency—a typically fatalist and pre-Enlightenment attitude, which is further reflected in the emotional tone of his writing. Moreover, his thoughts are expressed in the traditional meter of folk poetry, not in the prose of scientific scholarship or philosophical discourse. He also makes no attempt to broach the problem of cultural backwardness in the rationalist and utilitarian spirit of the Enlightenment that one finds in contemporary intellectuals, such as Iosepos Moisiodax.

Characteristic of the way Dapontes's oeuvre blends the two worlds of thought is also the large number of entertaining stories by Greek and Roman authors inserted as digressions within the main narrative of the *Garden of Graces*: "Pindus and the Serpent" by Claudius Aelianus; the story of the tyrant Polykrates by Herodotus; Plutarch's story of Timoclea of Thebes; Athenaeus of Naucrates's romance of Odatis and Zariadres; the controversial story of Combabus and Stratonice by Lucian; and tales from Ovid's *Metamorphoses*.[65] These lighthearted stories, all retold in rhyming couplets of fifteen-syllable verse, are akin in tone to other vernacular stories popular with Greek readers of the time—Croce's *Bertoldo*, the Φυλλάδα τοῦ Γαδάρου (*Story*

64 *Garden of Graces*, 11.35–114.
65 Dapontes considered Ovid's tales of metamorphoses to be the most "entertaining [and] worthy of laughter" (*Garden of Graces*, 15.301, 321–22, 395). The stories probably echoed the protean sense of his own identity.

of the Donkey), and the *Arabian Nights*, to name a few.[66] Unlike these, however, Dapontes's stories are all of classical origin, reflecting the growing interest in the literature of antiquity among an enlightened and western-influenced Greek readership.[67] Tellingly, Dapontes inserts these ancient stories in a work whose overt purpose was to celebrate a highly revered Orthodox relic. (He even inserts the more risqué of Ovid's stories in the chapter that recounts his return to Mount Athos, at the beginning of which he pledges to lead a life of repentance![68]) Dapontes was well aware that these racy tales would scandalize the more stern and hidebound of his Orthodox readers, which is why he tries to reassure them of his just intent: he argues that pagan stories are necessary because they intensify the faith of Christian readers by reminding them of their redemption from an "abominable religion."[69] This is sophistic reasoning, thinly veiled. Dapontes's true sentiments on the matter are couched in the ensuing metaphor, where he compares the different narratives in his book to a home's utensils: golden ones mix naturally with lesser ones made of silver, tin, iron, or clay.[70] Despite the explicit hierarchy in this metaphor and its biblical provenance,[71] it is implied that Christian and secular "narratives" coexist in his mindset in a harmonious and wholesome way. He displays a similar ideological syncretism in the *Mirror of Women*, in which he supplements the text's

[66] For more on Greek popular culture of this period, see Clogg 1980: 126–28 and, more recently, Athini 2010: 3–74.

[67] Dapontes's awareness of ancient Greek lineage is discussed further in Soulogiannis 1970 and Kitromilides 2013: 67–69.

[68] *Garden of Graces*, 15.1–42.

[69] Ibid., 15.397–402. Religious authorities fiercely denounced popular literature. Writing a few decades later, Nikodemos Hagioreites, the principal compiler of the Orthodox Church's canon laws, could not be more explicit: "Just as we must suppress heretical books, we must suppress erotic books, such as the 'Erotokritos,' 'Erophile,' 'Voskopoula,' and others. The same applies to humorous books and indecent ones, such as the 'Halima,' 'Bertoldos,' the tale of 'Spanos,' the 'Gaidaros,' and other similar ones" (Agapios and Nikodemos 1800: 49).

[70] *Garden of Graces*, 15.403–10.

[71] 2 Tim. 2:20.

religious material with passages drawn from ancient history and classical mythology.[72]

Perhaps the most elaborate expression of Dapontes's hybrid worldview is the "Canon of Hymns Containing Many Exceptional Things"—a work that has elicited wildly diverse responses among modern critics, from those who consider it a forerunner of Elytis's *Axion Esti*,[73] to those who perceive it as little more than a meaningless muddle.[74] The composition is modeled after the Byzantine Canon, a complex genre with origins in late-seventh-century monastic worship, which typically consists of nine odes, each containing a group of six to nine stanzas (*troparia*) that correspond thematically to as many biblical canticles from the Old Testament.[75] In composing his "Canon of Hymns," Dapontes retained the genre's form and structure (the number of odes, metrical pattern, and reference to the canticles) and replaced the traditional subject matter with an array of items that he personally considered worthy of admiration.[76] Although, strictly speaking, it is a parody of ecclesiastical hymns, falling within the long-standing tradition of parahymnology,[77] the work at no point evokes ridicule or irreverence. On the contrary, suspended between a sense of wonder and worship, it pays homage to the divine abundance of the earth.

As one would expect, the majority of the items mentioned are drawn from the wider world of Orthodox culture: icons, crosses,

---

[72] On the importance that Dapontes attached to secular historical knowledge, as evidenced in the *Mirror of Women*, see Kitromilides 2013: 67–70.

[73] Savvidis 1991a: 64.

[74] Angelou 1997: 81.

[75] The second ode was usually omitted, so the actual number was eight. For a thorough analysis of the structure, content, style, and development of the Byzantine Canon, see Skrekas 2008: vii–cxi.

[76] Dapontes was well acquainted with the genre since ecclesiastical Canons were part of the educational curriculum. He had also edited two liturgical texts and incorporated regular canonical hymns in other works (Sathas 1872: ξζ΄).

[77] Mitsakis 1990.

relics, as well as churches and monasteries located in Russia and the Balkans. However, these are cited alongside items belonging to other religious cultures ("St. Peter's in Rome," "the tomb of Mohammad," "the mosques of Constantinople") and next to admirable qualities of different ethnic groups ("French artistry," "Indian simplicity," and "Turkish hospitality," for instance). By doing so, Dapontes is clearly espousing the value of religious tolerance, which found particular expression during the early phase of the Greek Enlightenment.[78]

In the "Canon of Hymns" one also finds a strong echo of the contemporary interest in geography that was mentioned earlier. Dapontes refers to more than one hundred place names in Europe, Africa, and Asia, ranging from Spain to India and from Poland to Madagascar. By this grand geographical sweep he produces a verbal equivalent of the cartographic material found in contemporary sources, while his recurrent references to the Far East echo the Enlightenment interest in oriental and exotic cultures.[79] Undoubtedly, the "Canon of Hymns" also reflects the great trading boom of the time: it was published in 1778, four years after the treaty of Kucuk Kaynardi, which signaled the end of the Russo-Turkish war and guaranteed unprecedented rights to Greek merchants (Dapontes even makes a passing reference to this war in Ode IX.2).[80] The abundance of goods made available through this commercial expansion helps to explain the work's dazzling display of foods, spices, textiles, and wines. Many of these products, both local and foreign, were highly-prized commodities (Chinese musk and Moscovite furs, for example, as well as the less exotic but equally exclusive quinces of Adrianople and Athenian honey). As a catalog—more than two hundred items

[78] Voulgaris's well-known essay on religious tolerance is representative of this early Enlightenment period ([Voulgaris] 1768: 217–84; Manikas 2009).

[79] In his Κατάλογος ἱστορικός, Dapontes mentions that he was a keen reader of the history and culture of China (Sathas 1872: 111), which is the most frequently cited location in the "Canon of Hymns" after Wallachia, Venice, and Constantinople; the other eastern locations cited are India, Persia, and Arabia.

[80] Text references to the "Canon of Hymns" are to odes and stanzas.

are listed—the "Canon of Hymns" could also be said to embody the desire for encyclopedic knowledge, which defined the secular spirit of the age.[81] A kaleidoscope of worldly pleasures and sacred artifacts, of traditional sensibilities and modern thought, Dapontes's "Canon of Hymns" perfectly captures the cultural heterogeneity of his age.

Bursting with the sensuality of fragrances and the tastes of worldly goods, while at the same time expressing gratitude for what Dapontes perceived to be gifts of a divine creation, the "Canon of Hymns" presents an intimate interplay between spiritual vocation and secular engagement. One finds a similar entwinement in a letter of 1760 to a Phanariot dignitary, in which Dapontes matches Christian vices and virtues to individual foods laid on a table: "At the table I do not want loaves of theft, lambs of injustice ... or quails of resentment. ... I would rather there be loaves of sweat, lentils of humility, beans of prudence, chick peas of mercy, fish of simplicity, olives of mirth, and cabbage of piety. I want moral fables for starters and parables for dessert. Lay faith on the table in place of a salt shaker."[82] This blend is characteristic of Dapontes's life too, especially the period after his tonsure. For three years he lived in the solitude of a cell, dedicating his time to prayer and contemplation; for the next eight, he immersed himself in

---

[81] The "Canon of Hymns" is but one of the many lists and catalogs that feature in Dapontes's oeuvre, often contained within a larger work: in the "Geographical History," for example, there is a descriptive list of curious and "admirable" objects found in the royal palace in Copenhagen (Legrand 1880–88, 3:lviii–lxii); in "Ἄνθη νοητὰ" Dapontes lists hundreds of churches and monasteries in the Balkans dedicated to the Virgin Mary (Papadop[o]ulos-Kerameus 1909: 279–311); in the *Garden of Graces* he lists prominent monks and priests of Mount Athos (16.15–52), as well as the builders and benefactors of the Xeropotamou Monastery (8.161–220). He also compiled a list of more than a hundred churches, shrines, and monasteries found in his home island of Skopelos (Papadopoulos-Kerameus 1910). The same predilection for catalogs and lists underlies some of his works in their entirety: the *Mirror of Women*; the unpublished "Βίβλος βασιλειῶν" (Book of Emperors), a history of the emperors of Byzantium (Kechagioglou 2009); and the *Κατάλογος ἱστορικός*, an encyclopedic work recording prominent men and events of his time (Sathas 1872: 73–200).

[82] Legrand 1880–88, 1:υγ´.

the bustle of urban life, engaging in social and material exchanges. As
a missionary living among lay people, his inner calling was strength-
ened rather than questioned; as a hermit practicing ascetic discipline,
his worldly senses were heightened rather than numbed—both para-
doxes encapsulated in the much-quoted couplets:

The things I was deprived of in my youth
I relish now in old age as a monk.
The things I missed as layman, now as monk
I revel in, beyond all expectation.[83]

Dapontes had little of a monk's typical hardness and austerity
(Dawkins is quite right to imagine that his innocently hedonistic
temper would have been intolerable to ascetic types);[84] but this
innate capacity for joy did not make him any less spiritual.

Romantic Outsider, Spiritual Enlightener

An individual at once eccentric and representative of his age, at
once worldly and spiritual, Dapontes emerges as a highly elusive
figure. This elusiveness stems in part from his recurrent experiences
of exclusion, and one finds that these experiences were what fueled
his literary activity to a large extent: he began to cultivate his writing
talent when he suddenly found himself in Bucharest without political
contacts and as an outsider was subsequently shouldered aside. It was
thanks to this talent that he eventually found himself at the center of
Phanariot society. He began the *Mirror of Women* in prison, a further
instance of exclusion following his banishment in Crimea. (It is
not surprising that his favorite classical author was Ovid, famously

---

[83] "Ὅσα ἐγὼ στερεύθηκα νέος καὶ λαμπροφόρος, / τώρα ἐδῶ τ' ἀπόλαυσα γέρος καὶ
ρασοφόρος· / ὅσα δὲν εἶδα κοσμικός, καλόγηρος τὰ εἶδα, / κι ἐχάρηκα κι ἐχόρτασα
πᾶσαν μου παρ' ἐλπίδα" (*Garden of Graces*, 9.213–16). A similar sentiment is
expressed in 9.169–72.
[84] Dawkins 1936: 70.

exiled—like himself—to the distant shores of the Black Sea; and the dramatic dialogues that appear in the *Mirror of Women* may well be an echo of the dialogues found in demotic "songs of exile"). Similarly, he threw himself into a frenzy of writing activity after being ousted from the brotherhood on Piperi; in the seclusion of his cell he composed more than ten volumes of verse. Estranged and uprooted time and again, it was to writing that he would always turn, eventually discovering in it a radically new sense of belonging.

What adds to the peculiarity of Dapontes's oeuvre is a distinctly confessional voice, which was highly unusual for the literature of this period, yet unsurprising for a writer ostracized and isolated on so many occasions. This subjectivity is most evident in the *Garden of Graces*, in which he repeatedly reveals his private thoughts, expressing a sense of shame about his past and the need to atone for his "despicable" nature.[85] However much transformed he seemed by his new life as a monk, the worldliness of his former life continued to haunt him, giving rise to a nagging sense of inner conflict: he compares himself to a wolf whose "coat changes with age but remains wicked on the inside."[86] Elsewhere he likens himself to the mythological sea-god known for his continual changes:

I seemed different to the man I was within,
Appearing as a great ascetic
But, like Proteus the king, transformed myself
And took on many different forms.
(*Garden of Graces*, 12.11–14)

The confessional tone continues even at the end of the narrative when he purposely switches from a first- to a third-person account, signaling a sense of detachment as he feels his life drawing to a close. His sense of remorse persists:

85 *Garden of Graces*, 9.217–30.
86 Ibid., 5.25–26.

Here my wandering comes to an end
As does my narration
. . . .
The name "Kaisarios" is to be heard no more
. . . .
[He] laments his sins
That he committed in many cities and towns.
He sits in silence alone in his cell
And to God cries out with a sigh, "A sinner am I!"
. . . .
Such are his words as he sits and awaits
His death . . .
(*Garden of Graces*, 15.7–44)

This subjectivity is not found in the *Garden of Graces* alone or in the journal he kept thereafter.[87] Though otherwise detached and in line with the formality of religious writing, the majority of his works are peppered with private thoughts, feelings, and memories. These are expressed in the form of extended narratives, dramatic dialogues, or brief remarks. In the *Mirror of Women*, for instance, Dapontes interrupts the main narrative in order to reminisce about his time in Crimea or to recollect dreams from years past—digressions that seem to occur as spontaneously as the memories they describe.[88] He relates the events of his exile in the form of an imaginary dialogue between two personae (Psyche and Chariton) who signify his spiritual and worldly sides and help him come to terms with his inner conflict.[89] In the unpublished works "Φανάρι γυναικῶν" and "Βίβλος βασιλειῶν," he suspends

---

[87] Kadas 1988.

[88] *Mirror of Women*, 2:289–322, 400–406.

[89] Vivilakis 2013: 337–38. Such a spontaneous dramatic form may well echo the demotic songs of exile as well as ecclesiastical hymns (like the Akathist hymn), both of which incorporate dramatic dialogue at moments of highly charged tension (Dapontes was very familiar with both of them). I thank Caroline Makropoulos for drawing my attention to this point.

the main thread of the text to narrate personal incidents relating to his education or to his time in the Phanariot courts.[90] In his Πατερικὸν τοῦ ἐν ἁγίοις πατρὸς ἡμῶν Γρηγορίου τοῦ Διαλόγου πάπα Ῥώμης, a vernacular rendering of the sixth-century *Dialogues* of St. Gregory concerning the lives of the saints of Italy, he inserts a lengthy "Confessional Prayer" in which he pours out his deep-seated sense of sin: he presents various figures from the Old and New Testaments in typical catalog style, contrasting each of their virtues with his own transgressions.[91] The self repeatedly surfaces in this biblical survey as Dapontes tries "to describe in all truth who I really am,"[92] rendering the text a private place for his own soul-searching. Even in the "Canon of Hymns," he does not hesitate to allude to himself, including in his list of the world's most precious items "my own icon of the Mother of God."[93]

Few contemporary Greek writers injected such subjectivity into their writing—with the exception perhaps of the autobiographical writings of Patriarch Callinicus III (1713–1792), and of Iosepos Moisiodax whose Ἀπολογία (Apology) (1780), a defense of modern learning in the face of persecution, contains a fair amount of autobiographical material, though even in this exceptional case, the writer focuses on his intellectual career during his middle and later years, imparting precious little information about his early life.[94] Broadly speaking, the bulk of Greek writing in the eighteenth and early nineteenth centuries presented collective worldviews with little reference to the private world of individuals. This was to be expected in the case of religious and scientific writing, but it also applied to secular literature, such as neoclassical tragedies, satires, and sentimental fiction, where the reader has no sense of being privy to the charac-

[90] Vivilakis 2013: 327–28, and Kechagioglou 2009: 56, respectively.
[91] "Λόγος ἤ εὐχὴ ἐξαγορευτικὴ" (Confessional prayer), in Πατερικόν . . . , pp. 478–543.
[92] "Εἰς ἕνα δίστιχο νὰ πῶ ἀνελλιπῶς τελείως, / νὰ περιγράψω τίς εἰμι, καὶ ἀληθῶς κυρίως" (ibid., p. 537).
[93] "Canon of Hymns," VII.3.
[94] Angelou 1976; Kitromilides 1992: 17–127. On Callinicus III, see Tselikas 2004.

ters' inner thoughts. It was in the course of the next century, with
the rise of nationalism and the influence of Romanticism, that auto-
biographies, first-person narratives, and the private voice of the poet
made their appearance. Seen in this light, Dapontes's voice may be
interpreted as the expression of a rudimentary Romantic outlook. As
a case in point, one may note the description of his solitary ramblings
along the banks of a river and his emotions while contemplating
the beauty of the natural world.[95] Parallels have already been drawn
with his contemporary Rousseau (1712–1778), the embodiment of
the Romantic spirit, who was no less a wanderer than Dapontes.[96]
(He crossed the Alps on foot and incorporated his reflections in the
Confessions). One may also discern in Dapontes's writings the idea
of the authorial voice as well as an anxiety concerning the aesthetic
integrity of one's work—both distinctly Romantic sensibilities.
These are especially evident in the impassioned "Notice" added at the
end of Λόγοι πανηγυρικοί (*Panegyrics*), which appears here in trans-
lation. In this, Dapontes rants against plagiarists who "adorn them-
selves with the beauty of others" and censures careless copyists who
have "deformed" his work by stripping away "its original essence and
grace." Some of his verses may even be said to foreshadow the voice of
the anguished artist and Romantic notions of the creative self:

Woe betide those who are corrupters of books,
May they suffer God's wrath, as corrupters of children!
For like one's own offspring
The writer, the poet, cares for his books.
As a father suffers the pain of his children,
So a writer suffers for his compositions.[97]

95 *Mirror of Women*, 2:299–301.
96 See, for example, Angelou 1997: 25, 114.
97 "Κακόχρονον νὰ ἔχουσιν ὡς χαλασταὶ βιβλίων, / νὰ τοὺς χαλάσῃ ὁ θεός, ὡς
χαλαστὰς παιδίων! / ὅτι ὡς τέκνα, ὡς παιδιὰ λέγω τῇ ἀληθείᾳ, / ὁ συγγραφεὺς ὁ ποιητὴς
τὰ ἔχει τὰ βιβλία, / καὶ ὡς πονεῖ ἕνας πατὴρ πάσχοντα τὰ παιδιά του, / οὕτω πονεῖ καὶ
συγγραφεὺς γιὰ τὰ συγγράμματά του" ("Geographical History," in Sathas 1872: νε´).

The creative solitude that Dapontes often experienced not only
encourages one to regard the man as a forerunner of the Romantic
sensibilities that were to follow the age of Enlightenment; but it also
invites one to connect him with hesychasm, a spiritual movement often
overlooked in studies of eighteenth-century Greek culture. Hesychasm
was an early monastic tradition of silent, contemplative prayer, whose
practitioners aimed at attaining communion with God. It had fallen
into decline since the fourteenth century, but in Dapontes's time was
regaining popularity on Mount Athos (not without a degree of contro-
versy), as religious leaders attempted to counteract the growing laxity
of ritual traditions and remedy what was perceived as the spiritual
atrophy of the Church brought on by centuries of scholastic teaching.[98]
It may seem strange to connect an individual known for verbosity and
an epicurean temperament with a practice that called for total silence
and self-denial. Yet despite his proverbial wordiness and hearty appe-
tite, Dapontes was intrigued by such extreme forms of asceticism. His
spiritual sensibility, which began during his childhood on Skopelos
(prayer was one of "the three foundations" of his happiness) and was
reawakened during his exile in Crimea, eventually led to monastic
vows and a life of complete silence for three years.[99] His "Encomium
of Solitude and the Monastic Life," written after this extended
retreat, is the testimony of a soul struggling to achieve communion
with God through still and silent prayer.[100] On his mission he claims
to have reached moments of transcendent and holistic joy, which
appear similar to the sense of rapture that sometimes accompanied
the hesychast way of life.[101] His admiration for cave hermits and cave
monasteries, mentioned repeatedly in his writings, is another unmis-
takable case in point.[102] Equally importantly, Dapontes was a profound

[98] Ware 2005: 71. On the religious controversy associated with the revival of
hesychasm, see Patapios and Chrysostomos 2006: 27–45.
[99] "Ζῶντας κατὰ ἀλήθειαν μὲ ἄκραν ἡσυχίαν" (*Garden of Graces*, 5.45).
[100] Ibid., 5.137–218.
[101] Ibid., 9.173–76.
[102] *Mirror of Women*, 2:303; *Garden of Graces*, 11.215–22, 263–72; "Canon of

admirer of the *Philokalia* (1782), a weighty anthology of hesychast texts, widely regarded today as the most important Orthodox spiritual work produced during Ottoman rule.[103]

It may seem incongruous to connect a man who was receptive to Enlightenment thought with the hesychasm—a movement which, in the latter part of the eighteenth century, was greatly hostile to the ideas and supporters of the Enlightenment. In the aftermath of the French Revolution, when the radical implications of a similar upheaval against Ottoman rule were becoming increasingly apparent, it was the supporters of hesychasm, such as Nikodemos Hagioreitis and Athanasios Parios, who were the most outspoken reactionaries against the liberal ideas of western Europe; the Orthodox tradition of hesychasm afforded the best antidote against "the venomous atheism of the West" and the looming emergence of a secular neo-Hellenic identity.[104] Propaganda, persecution, and polemical pamphlets spread like wildfire in the decades that followed. The two movements were at odds on a philosophical level too: hesychasm aimed at achieving a union of heart (καρδία) and mind (νοῦς), while the Enlightenment championed the cause of reason alone, driving a wedge between the intellectual and metaphysical faculties of man.[105] There is nothing

Hymns," VII.5.

[103] Ware 2005, 72; Kitromilides 2000: 341. The compilers of the *Philokalia* were the two leading figures of the hesychast movement, Nikodemos Hagioreitis and Makarios Notaras. Dapontes writes in the Κατάλογος ἱστορικός: "[Makarios Notaras of Corinth] encouraged two merchants to publish two valuable and large books, the *Philokalia* and the *Euergetinon*, which he had brought over from Mount Athos. Both books are most beneficial to the soul, especially the *Philokalia*, which ought not to be called a book at all but a library, since it contains the writings of many Holy Fathers; may God grant him a long life" (Sathas 1872: 109). Dapontes's interest in hesychasm may also be connected to his stay in Moldavian monasteries during his mission: hesychasm was prevalent in them in the early part of the eighteenth century (Ware 2005: 105).

[104] For a useful overview of conservatives' reaction to the Enlightenment, see Kitromilides 2006: 205–9.

[105] Louth 2003.

to suggest, however, that Dapontes was ill at ease in entertaining
Enlightenment ideas while remaining true to his hesychast calling.
Although on occasions he echoed messianic prophecies about the
rebirth of Byzantium,[106] he was voicing entrenched hopes shared
by Orthodox subjects for years, rather than making an implicit
statement against western liberalism.[107] In fact, he never demon-
strated any of the prejudice or parochialism displayed by reactionary
Orthodox thinkers.[108] On the contrary, with his altogether encyclo-
pedic outlook, he was receptive to new lines of inquiry in fields such
as geography, history, and the literature of antiquity. Had Dapontes
lived long enough to witness the escalation of the conflict in the after-
math of the French Revolution, it is unlikely that he would have taken
a polemical stance against either side. Since becoming a monk, he
had categorically distanced himself from political affairs; for him, the
appeal of hesychasm lay chiefly in its spiritual rather than in its ideo-
logical potential.

One might add that the spirituality of hesychasm even permeated
his writings, for Dapontes was able, through silence, to tune into the
sacredness of language itself. At the time of writing the *Garden of
Graces* (1768), he described the joy and gratitude he felt on Piperi
as ineffable (5.126), a nod perhaps to the apophatic tradition of
Christian mysticism to which hesychasm belonged. By the time of
the "Canon of Hymns" (1778), however, the poet reaffirms his faith

---

[106] *Κατάλογος ἱστορικός* (Sathas 1872: 119–20); Hatzopoulos 2009: 84–85.

[107] On the prophecies of "Agathangelos," which were prevalent in the popular
culture of the period, see Clogg 1980: 128–30.

[108] For the contrasting attitudes to the second-century satirist Lucian, whose recep-
tion has often been used by critics as a yardstick for evaluating cultural ideologies,
see Goldhill 2002: 5–6. To conservatives, Lucian was anathema. Athanasios Parios
called him "filthy and despicable" ([Parios] 1805: 133); and Nikodemos Hagioreites
denounced him as an "atheist" whose "mythologies are deadly and detrimental to
the soul" (Nikodemos 1803: 96). Dapontes, on the other hand, had no qualms about
including in his *Garden of Graces* some of Lucian's stories, and some rather racy ones
at that (16.681ff.). He also translated four of Lucian's dialogues, which appear in his
Χρηστοήθεια ... (Christian morality ...) (1770); see Cerenzia 1975/76.

in the power of language—not as a signifier that would challenge
apophatic knowledge but as a participant in a sacramental exchange
that could reinforce its very sacredness. Just as in the sacrament of the
Eucharist the priest gives thanks for creation by offering back to God
the fruits of the earth with the stamp of human creativity, Dapontes
gives his thanks by reshaping not wheat into bread or grapes into wine
but language itself.[109] He arranges the words to produce an incanta-
tory pattern of sounds (aptly described by one critic as "a musical
string of beads"),[110] an acoustic abundance that complements other
sensual delights—sights, smells, textures and tastes—summoned in
the hymns as a manifestation of God's plenitude.[111] Quite literally, he
offers to the Mother of God, in return for the cornucopia of exquisite
things he feels humbled to behold, a "gift of words" ("λογικὰ δῶρα").
Dapontes's "Canon of Hymns" may be a faithful snapshot of contem-
porary culture but it is equally a timeless expression of faith in the
bounty of God and the sacred power of language.

An individual who lived for the most part in the margins of his
society, Dapontes resists being classified into any one of the social
groups commonly associated with the Greek world of the eighteenth

[109] On the sacrament of the Eucharist, Ware writes: "When . . . we offer back to
God the first fruits of the earth, we offer them not in their original form but reshaped
by the hand of man: we bring to the altar not sheaves of wheat but loaves of bread,
not grapes but wine. So man is priest of the creation through his power to give thanks
and to offer the creation back to God" (Ware 1995: 54).

[110] Savvidis 1991a: 65.

[111] One could note, for example the consonance in "Παντζέχρι σκαντζοχοίρου
. . . Τριαντάφυλλα Φράντζας καὶ ἀντζόγαις . . . τζίροι τ᾽ Ἀριτζιοῦ" (Ode III); the allit-
eration in "τοξάρια τὰ Τατάρικα" (Ode IV), "περιβόλια τοῦ Παρισιοῦ καὶ παλάτια"
(Ode VI), and "Μωάμεθ τὸ μνῆμα καὶ οἱ μαῦροι" (Ode VIII); the alliteration and
rhyme in "τοῦ Νείλου πλημμύρα καὶ καταρράκται καὶ πηγαί, Εὐρίππου, Εὐφράτου τε,
Τίγριδος παλίρροιαι" (Ode VIII); and the assonance in "Ταραμπουλοῦσι σαπούνιον . .
. τουτοῦνι" (Ode IV) and "λουτρὰ τῆς Προύσας" (Ode VIII).

century: the Phanariot elite, Enlightenment intellectuals, bourgeois merchants, conservative monks and clerics of the Orthodox Church, or the broad mass of rural folk. Looking back over his life as a whole, we find that while connected to each of these groups in different ways and to varying degrees, he never committed himself wholeheartedly to any single one of them. He lived for fifteen years among the Phanariots, only to turn his back on that world in later life; he was well acquainted with the culture of modern learning but never joined the ranks of the Enlightenment intelligentsia; he was deeply influenced by the revival of Orthodox spirituality but never became a politically active defender of the Church; he was always mindful of his rural origins yet did not return to his home island (save for a short stay in later life), preferring to fashion himself as an ecumenical inhabitant.

An elusive and composite individual, Dapontes may finally seem more at home in fiction—not such an unreasonable suggestion, given how often Dapontes shaped his identity through writing. Interestingly enough, he bears a striking similarity to one of the characters in Voltaire's *Candide* (1759), a work published only a few years before the *Garden of Graces* was written. In this philosophical *conte*, the doyen of the French Enlightenment hoped to expose the absurdity of a worldview governed solely by rationalism, resolving Candide's deadlock at the end of the story through the character of the *bon vieillard*—a kind old man living contentedly on a small plot of land on the outskirts of Constantinople. Like Dapontes on Piperi, this humble and otherworldly figure spends his time tending the crops in his garden and enjoying the fruits of his labor while steering clear of the vanity and vices attendant on those who are driven by power and ambition. Moved by this old man's simplicity, the long-suffering Candide finally frees himself from the relentless rationalism and wildly optimistic ideas of his tutor Pangloss as soon as he commits to cultivating his own garden. He chooses silence over speculation ("Let us work without reasoning" is his new maxim). In his garden, Candide is no longer dispirited by the limitations of human understanding or by the agony of existence, both previously compensated for by an overarching philosophical system; instead, he transforms these into a new way of life marked by silence, creativity, and a taste for "oranges and nuts"—quite like Dapontes in his own "garden of graces," where he was blissfully content with his almonds and leeks and where he found his true vocation in the ecumenical order of things. Perhaps it was this holistic vision which enabled him to embrace many seemingly conflicting points of view.

Coincidentally, in an early nineteenth-century anthology of Phanariot poetry, Dapontes's long poem "Περὶ ματαιότητος κόσμου καὶ ἀθλιότητος τοῦ ἀνθρώπου" ("On the Vanity of the World and the Woes of Man") appears next to a verse translation of another conte by Voltaire, *Memnon, or Human Wisdom*—a work which, like *Candide*, exposes the folly of the overweening philosopher.[112] In his poem, Dapontes alerts his readers to the fragility of life and the immanence of death, bewailing the vain seekers of earthly power (their "gold-harnessed horses and purple-covered carriages" clearly an allusion to the flamboyant lifestyle of Phanariot *hospodars*, to whom the poem was originally addressed). Without being explicit, Dapontes would have glimpsed the vanity of a philosophical system which, in setting out to put man on the path of progress through an excessive, if not exclusive, reliance on reason, unwittingly stripped life of its sacredness and daily enchantment. Writing in the spirit of Ecclesiastes, Dapontes sensed that humanity was no more than a flower that "blooms, then fades and quickly shrivels up." However, the futility that he saw was not in creation itself, whose diversity he exalted and wrote about with such rapture, but in the abstractions and ambitions that blinded one to its beauty. A man intensely in the world and at the same time outside it, Dapontes was able to embody the diversity that defined the culture of the Greek-speaking world in the eighteenth century, while recording a passion in a body of writing that may continue to divide critics but will rarely fail to charm.

---

[112] Daoutis 1818: 40–56; Frantzi 1993: 51–73, 93–118.

References

Greek titles and publishers' names appear below in polytonic or monotonic Greek, depending on the orthography of the original publications.

Agapios, Hieromonachos, and Monachos Nikodemos [Nikodemos Hagioreites]. 1800. *Πηδάλιον τῆς νοητῆς νηός, τῆς μίας, ἁγίας, καθολικῆς καὶ ἀποστολικῆς τῶν ὀρθοδόξων ἐκκλησίας.* Leipzig: Breitkopf & Härtel.

Angelomati-Tsounkaraki, Eleni. 2000. "Ἑλληνικὰ περιηγητικὰ κείμενα (16ος–19ος αἰ.)." *Μεσαιωνικὰ καὶ Νέα Ἑλληνικὰ* 6:155–80.

———. 2007. "Τὸ φαινόμενο τῆς ζητείας κατὰ τὴ μεταβυζαντινὴ περίοδο." *Ἰόνιος Λόγος* 1:247–93.

———. 2010. "Ἕνα λανθάνον ἔργο τοῦ Καισάριου Δαπόντε καὶ ἡ ἁγιοποίηση τοῦ Πελοποννήσιου Ἱερόθεου τοῦ Ἰβηρίτη." *Ἰόνιος Λόγος* 2:1–11.

Angelou, Alkis, ed. 1976. *Ἀπολογία.* By Iosepos Moisiodax. Athens: Ἑρμῆς.

———. 1988. "Ἡ δίκη τοῦ Μεθόδιου Ἀνθρακίτη (ὅπως τὴν ἀφηγεῖται ὁ ἴδιος)." In *Τῶν Φώτων: Ὄψεις τοῦ Νεοελληνικοῦ Διαφωτισμοῦ,* 23–37. Νεοελληνικὰ μελετήματα, n.s., 9. Athens: Ἑρμῆς.

———, ed. 1997. *Κῆπος χαρίτων.* By Kaisarios Dapontes. Athens: Ἑστία.

Athini, Stesi. 2010. *Ὄψεις της νεοελληνικής αφηγηματικής πεζογραφίας, 1700–1830: Ο διάλογος με τις ελληνικές και ξένες παραδόσεις στη θεωρία και στην πράξη.* Athens: Εθνικό Ἵδρυμα Ερευνών, Ινστιτούτο Νεοελληνικών Ερευνών.

Bouchard, Jacques. 1982. "Nicolas Mavrocordatos et l'aube des Lumières." *Revue des Études Sud-Est Européennes* 20:237–46.

Camariano-Cioran, Ariadna. 1974. *Les académies princières de Bucarest et de Jassy et leurs professeurs.* Thessaloniki: Institute for Balkan Studies.

Cavarnos, Constantine. 1985. *St. Cosmas Aitolos.* 3rd ed. Modern Orthodox Saints, vol. 1. Belmont, MA: Institute for Byzantine and Modern Greek Studies.

Cerenzia, Vera. 1975/76. "Dapontes traduttore di Luciano." *Rivista di Studi Bizantini e Neoellenici,* n.s., 12/13:161–73.

Clanton, Dan W. 2006. *The Good, the Bold, and the Beautiful: The Story of Susanna and Its Renaissance Interpretations.* New York: T&T Clark.

Clogg, Richard. 1980. "Elite and Popular Culture in Greece under Turkish Rule." In *Hellenic Perspectives: Essays in the History of Greece,* edited by John T. A. Koumoulides, 107–43. Lanham, MD: University Press of America.

Costache, Ştefania. 2010/11. "Loyalty and Political Legitimacy in the Phanariots' Historical Writing in the Eighteenth Century." *Südost-Forschungen* 69/70: 25–50.

Daoutis, Zisis, ed. 1818. *Διάφορα ἠθικὰ καὶ ἀστεῖα στιχουργήματα.* Vienna: Johann Barth[olomäus] Zweck.

Dawkins, R. M. 1936. *The Monks of Athos.* London: George Allen & Unwin.

Deligiannis, G. 1936. "Καισαρίου Δαπόντε ἐπιστολαὶ πρὸς τὸν Πατριάρχην Καλλίνικον Γ΄." Pt. 1. *Θεολογία* 14:70–71.

———. 1937. "Καισαρίου Δαπόντε ἐπιστολαὶ πρὸς τὸν Πατριάρχην Καλλίνικον Γ΄." Pts. 2 and 3. *Θεολογία* 15:155–58; 269–72.

Erbiceanu, Constantin, ed. 1888. *Cronicariĭ grecĭ cariĭ au scris despre românĭ în epoca fanariotă.* Bucharest: Tipografia Cărţilor Bisericesci.

Frantzi, Anteia, ed. 1993. *Μισμαγιά: Ἀνθολόγιο φαναριώτικης ποίησης κατὰ τὴν ἔκδοση Ζήση Δαούτη (1818).* Athens: Ἑστία.

Galitis, Georgios A. 1975. "Ἄγνωστος αὐτόγραφος κώδιξ τοῦ Κωνσταντίνου-Καισαρίου Δαπόντε," *Ἐπιστημονική Ἐπετηρίδα Θεολογικῆς Σχολῆς Θεσσαλονίκης* 20: 5–41.

Gedeon, Manouel I. 1885. *Ὁ Ἄθως: Ἀναμνήσεις, ἔγγραφα, σημειώσεις.* Constantinople: Ἐκ τοῦ Πατριαρχικοῦ Τυπογραφείου.

Goldhill, Simon. 2002. *Who Needs Greek? Contests in the Cultural History of Hellenism.* Cambridge: Cambridge University Press.

Gounaridis, Paris. 1993. *Αρχείο της Ιεράς Μονής Ξηροποτάμου: επιτομές μεταβυζαντινών εγγράφων.* Αθωνικά Σύμμεικτα 3. Athens: Εθνικό Ίδρυμα Ερευνών, Κέντρο Βυζαντινών Ερευνών.

Hatzopoulos, Marios. 2009. "From Resurrection to Insurrection: 'Sacred' Myths, Motifs, and Symbols in the Greek War of Independence." In *The Making of Modern Greece: Nationalism, Romanticism, and the Uses of the Past (1797–1896)*, edited by Roderick Beaton and David Ricks, 81–93. Farnham, UK: Ashgate.

Kadas, Soterios N. 1988. "Χειρόγραφο με αυτόγραφες σημειώσεις του Καισάριου Δαπόντε." In *Αφιέρωμα στον Εμμανουήλ Κριαρά: Πρακτικά επιστημονικού συμποσίου, 3 Απριλίου 1987*, edited by I. Tarnanidis, G. Lavvas, E. Tsolakis, Ch. Papastathis, and P. Asimakopoulou-Atzaka, 181–235. Thessaloniki: Αριστοτέλειο Πανεπιστήμιο Θεσσαλονίκης, Κέντρο Βυζαντινών Ερευνών.

Kallianos, Konstantinos N. 1987. "Ανέκδοτα σημειώματα του Καισαρίου Δαπόντε για τη νήσο Σκόπελο (1778–1784)." *Ο Εφημέριος* 36 n.13, 274–78.

Kamarianou, Ariadne. 1959. "Λαϊκὰ τραγούδια καὶ φαναριώτικα στιχουργήματα Ἑλλήνων καὶ Ρουμάνων τοῦ 18ου καὶ 19ου αἰῶνος." *Λαογραφία* 18:94–112.

Kaplanis, Tassos A. 2001. "Women in the Looking-Glass: The Philogynous Dapontes (1713–1784) within the Misogynous Tradition of the Middle Ages." *Σύγκριση / Comparaison / Comparison* 12:48–70.

Karanasios, Chariton. 2016. "Το άγνωστο έργο του Καισαρίου Δαπόντε Βρύσις λογική (1778): Επιστολαί εκ της φυλακής και κατά των Κολυβάδων." Μεσαιωνικά και Νέα Ελληνικά 12: 255–387.

Kechagioglou, Giorgos. 1986. "Ανέκδοτα στοιχεία για τον Καισάριο Δαπόντε από το χειρόγραφο της Βυτίνας αριθ. 1." Ερανιστής 18:35–56.

———. 2009. "Η ιστοριογραφία ως όχημα συνειρμικής συναφήγησης και εγκιβωτιστικής παρέκβασης: Το λογοτεχνικό παράδειγμα της ασύμμετρα διασκεδαστικής 'Βίβλου Βασιλειών' του Καισάριου Δαπόντε." In Realia Byzantina, edited by Sofia Kotzabassi and Giannis Mavromatis, 47–56. Byzantinisches Archiv, vol. 22. Berlin: Walter de Gruyter.

Kitromilides, Paschalis M. 1992. The Enlightenment as Social Criticism: Iosipos Moisiodax and Greek Culture in the Eighteenth Century. Princeton, NJ: Princeton University Press.

———. 1996a. "Athos and the Enlightenment." In Mount Athos and Byzantine Monasticism: Papers from the Twenty-Eighth Spring Symposium of Byzantine Studies, Birmingham, March 1994, edited by Anthony Bryer and Mary Cunningham, 257–72. Society for the Promotion of Byzantine Studies 4. Aldershot, UK: Variorum. Reprinted with the original pagination in Kitromilides 2007.

———. 1996b. "'Balkan Mentality': History, Legend, Imagination." Nations and Nationalism 2:163–91. Reprinted with the original pagination in Kitromilides 2007.

———. 2000. "Philokalia's First Journey?" In Ενθύμησις Νικολάου Μ. Παναγιωτάκη, edited by Stephanos Kaklamanis, Athanasios Markopoulos, and Giannis Mavromatis, 341–60. Irakleio: Πανεπιστημιακές Εκδόσεις Κρήτης / Βικελαία Δημοτική Βιβλιοθήκη Ηρακλείου. Reprinted with the original pagination in Kitromilides 2007.

———. 2006. "Orthodoxy and the West: Reformation to Enlightenment." In *The Cambridge History of Christianity*, vol. 5, *Eastern Christianity*, edited by Michael Angold, 187–209. Cambridge: Cambridge University Press.

———. 2007. *An Orthodox Commonwealth: Symbolic Legacies and Cultural Encounters in Southeastern Europe*. Variorum Collected Studies. Aldershot, UK: Ashgate.

———. 2013. *Enlightenment and Revolution: The Making of Modern Greece*. Cambridge, MA: Harvard University Press.

Koumarianou, Aikaterine, ed. 1988. Γεωγραφία νεωτερική. By Daniel Philippides and Grigorios Konstantas. Athens: Ἑρμῆς.

Legrand, Émile, ed. 1880–88. "Δακικαὶ ἐφημερίδες."... By Konstantinos Dapontes. 3 vols. Paris: Ernest Leroux.

———, ed. 1881. *Bibliothèque grecque vulgaire*. Vol. 3. Paris: Maisonneuve.

Louth, Andrew. 2003. "The Theology of the *Philokalia*." In *Abba: The Tradition of Orthodoxy in the West; Festschrift for Bishop Kallistos (Ware) of Diokleia*, edited by John Behr, Andrew Louth, and Dimitri Conomos, 351–61. Crestwood, NY: St. Vladimir's Seminary Press.

Mackridge, Peter. 1981. "The Greek Intelligentsia, 1780–1830: A Balkan Perspective." In *Balkan Society in the Age of Greek Independence*, edited by Richard M. Clogg, 63–84. London: Macmillan.

———. 1994. "The Return of the Muses: Some Aspects of Revivalism in Greek Literature, 1760–1840." Κάμπος: *Cambridge Papers in Modern Greek* 2:47–71.

Manikas, Konstantinos I. 2009. Εὐγένιος Βούλγαρης καὶ ἀνεξιθρησκεία: Ἱστορικὴ καὶ θεολογικὴ προσέγγιση. Athens: Παρρησία.

Mazower, Mark. 2001. *The Balkans: From the End of Byzantium to the Present Day*. London: Phoenix Press.

Minaoglou, Charalambos A. 2007. "Greek Travelers and Travel Literature from the Fifteenth to the Eighteenth Century." In *Greek Research in Australia: Proceedings of the Sixth Biennial International Conference of Greek Studies, Flinders University, June 2005,* edited by Elizabeth Close, Michael Tsianikas, and George Couvalis, 305–12. Adelaide: Flinders University, Department of Languages.

Mitsakis, K. 1990. "Byzantine and Modern Greek Parahymnography." In *Studies in Eastern Chant,* vol. 5, edited by Dimitri Conomos, 9–76. Crestwood, NY: St. Vladimir's Seminary Press.

Nikodemos Hagioreites. 1803. Βιβλίον καλούμενον Χρηστοήθεια τῶν Χριστιανῶν. Venice: Ἐν τῇ Τυπογραφίᾳ Νικολάου Γλυκύ.

Paizi-Apostolopoulou, Machi. 2004. "Ἀναζητώντας τα όρια μιας πνευματικής ιδιοποίησης. Θύμα ή θύτης ο Κωνσταντίνος Δαπόντες;" In *Μνήμη Ἀλκη Αγγέλου: τα άθφονα σχήματα του παρελθόντος,* 429–36. Thessalonike: University Studio Press.

——————. 2007a. "Πῶς ὁ Κωνσταντίνος Δαπόντες ἔγινε Καισάριος: Τὸ τέλος τοῦ ἐγκόσμιου βίου του." In *Ἕλληνες λόγιοι τοῦ 18ου αἰώνα, ἀφανεῖς, ἄσημοι καὶ διάσημοι, σὲ διασταυρούμενες τροχιές: Βαρνάβας ὁ Κύπριος, Δημήτριος Ραμαδάνης, Καισάριος Δαπόντες, Νικόλαος Καρατζάς,* 113–33. Athens: Ἐθνικὸ Ἴδρυμα Ἐρευνῶν, Κέντρο Νεοελληνικῶν Ἐρευνῶν.

——————. 2007b. "Ἡ βιβλιοθήκη τοῦ Νικολάου Καρατζᾶ καὶ ἡ περιπέτεια τοῦ χειρογράφου Paris. Suppl. gr. 1375." In *Ἕλληνες λόγιοι τοῦ 18ου αἰώνα, ἀφανεῖς, ἄσημοι καὶ διάσημοι, σὲ διασταυρούμενες τροχιές: Βαρνάβας ὁ Κύπριος, Δημήτριος Ραμαδάνης, Καισάριος Δαπόντες, Νικόλαος Καρατζάς,* 137–63. Athens: Ἐθνικὸ Ἴδρυμα Ἐρευνῶν, Κέντρο Νεοελληνικῶν Ἐρευνῶν.

Papadop[o]ulos-Kerameus, A., ed. 1909. *Texte greceşti privitoare la istoria romanească. Vol. 13 of Documente privitoare la istoria romanilor. . . .* Bucharest: Ministerul Cultelor şi Instrucţiei Publice/Academia Română.

Papadopoulos-Kerameus, A. 1910. "Ναοί και μοναστήρια, εξωκλήσια και μονύδρια εν Σκοπέλω." *Byzantinische Zeitschrift* 19:91–96.

Papadopoulos-Vretos, Andreas. 1854. *Νεοελληνικὴ φιλολογία· ἤτοι, κατάλογος τῶν ἀπὸ πτώσεως τῆς Βυζαντινῆς Αὐτοκρατορίας μέχρι ἐγκαθιδρύσεως τῆς ἐν Ἑλλάδι βασιλείας τυπωθέντων βιβλίων παρ᾽ Ἑλλήνων εἰς τὴν ὁμιλουμένην, ἤ εἰς τὴν ἀρχαίαν ἑλληνικὴν γλῶσσαν.* . . . Pt. 1. Athens: Τύποις καὶ ἀναλώμασι Λ. Δ. Βηλαρᾶ καὶ Β. Π. Λιούμη.

[Parios, Athanasios]. 1805. *Ἀπολογία χριστιανική.* . . . Leipzig: [Johann Gotthilf] Neubert. Originally published as *Χριστιανικὴ ἀπολογία* (Constantinople: Ἐν τῷ τοῦ Πατριαρχείου τῆς Κωνσταντινουπόλεως Τυπογραφείῳ, 1798).

Paschalides, Symeon A., ed. 2012. *Ἡ αὐτόγραφη νεομαρτυρολογικὴ συλλογὴ τοῦ μοναχοῦ Καισαρίου Δαπόντε (1713–1784).* Thessaloniki: Μυγδονία.

Patapios, Hieromonk, and Archbishop Chrysostomos. 2006. *Manna from Athos: The Issue of Frequent Communion on the Holy Mountain in the Late Eighteenth and Early Nineteenth Centuries.* Byzantine and Neohellenic Studies 2. Oxford: Peter Lang.

Patapios Kausokalyvitis. 2008. "Ἡ Μονὴ Εὐαγγελιστρίας Σκοπέλου καὶ ὁ ἀνέκδοτος περὶ αὐτὴν κώδικας τοῦ μοναχοῦ Καισαρίου Δαπόντε." In *Ἀλεξανδρινὸς Ἀμητός: Ἀφιέρωμα στὴ μνήμη τοῦ Ι. Μ. Χατζηφώτη,* edited by M. G. Varvounis and Pan. Tzoumerkas, 2:455–76. Πηγὲς καὶ τεκμήρια πατριαρχικῆς ἱστορίας 3. Alexandreia: Πατριαρχικὴ Βιβλιοθήκη τοῦ Πατριαρχείου Ἀλεξανδρείας.

Polyviou, Miltiades D. 1992. "Ἡ ζητεία τοῦ Καισάριου Δαπόντε γιὰ τὴν ἀνοικοδόμηση τοῦ καθολικοῦ τῆς Μονῆς Ξηροποτάμου." *Κληρονομία* 24:183–203.

———. 1996. "Ὁ Καισάριος Δαπόντες καὶ οἱ ἀπεικονίσεις νεομαρτύρων στο καθολικό τῆς Μονῆς Ξηροποτάμου." *Ἑλληνικά* 46:115–25.

―――. 1999. *Το καθολικό της Μονής Ξηροποτάμου: Σχεδιασμός και κατασκευή στη ναοδομία του 18ου αιώνα*. Athens: Υπουργείο Πολιτισμού.

Sathas, Konstantinos N. 1868. *Νεοελληνικὴ φιλολογία: Βιογραφίαι τῶν ἐν τοῖς γράμμασι διαλαμψάντων Ἑλλήνων, ἀπὸ τῆς καταλύσεως τῆς Βυζαντινῆς Αὐτοκρατορίας μέχρι τῆς ἑλληνικῆς ἐθνεγερσίας (1453–1821)*. Athens: Ἐκ τῆς Τυπογραφίας τῶν τέκνων Ἀνδρέου Κορομηλᾶ.

―――, ed. 1872. *Μεσαιωνικὴ βιβλιοθήκη*. Vol. 3. Venice: Τύποις τοῦ Χρόνου.

Savvidis, G. P., ed. 1991a. *Κωνσταντίνου Δαπόντε, "Κανὼν περιεκτικὸς πολλῶν ἐξαιρέτων πραγμάτων τῶν εἰς πολλὰς πόλεις, καὶ νήσους, καὶ ἔθνη, καὶ ζῶα, ἐγνωσμένων" (1778)*. Athens: Λέσχη.

―――. 1991b. "Στοιχειώδεις πίνακες για την μελέτη Φαναριωτών ποιητών και στιχουργών." *Μολυβδοκονδυλοπελεκητής* 3:31–53.

―――, ed. 1993. *Κωνσταντίνου Δαπόντε, "Η θυσία του Ιεφθάε" και "Ιστορία Σωσάννης": Δύο συνεχόμενες συνθέσεις από τον "Καθρέπτη γυναικών."* Athens: Ιστός.

―――, ed. 1995a. *Κῆπος χαρίτων*. . . . By Konstantinos Kaisarios Dapontes. Athens: Ερμής.

―――. 1995b. "Παρατηρήσεις στην αφηγηματική τεχνική του Καισάριου Δαπόντε." In *Βουκόλεια: Mélanges offerts à Bertrand Bouvier*, edited by Anastasia Danaé Lazarides, Vincent Barras, and Terpsichore Birchler, 247–64. [Geneva]: Édition des Belles-Lettres.

Skrekas, Dimitrios. 2008. "Studies in the Iambic Canons Attributed to John of Damascus: A Critical Edition with Introduction and Commentary." D.Phil. thesis, University of Oxford.

Sophoklis, Gavriil, ed. 1880. *Κῆπος χαρίτων*. . . . By Konstantinos Kaisarios Dapontes. Athens: Ἐκ τοῦ Τυπογραφείου Ἑρμοῦ.

Soulogiannis, Euthymios. 1970. "Ὁ Δαπόντες, ἡ ἀντίληψίς του περὶ ἱστορίας καὶ ὁ πρόλογος εἰς τὸ 'Φανάρι γυναικῶν.'" Παρνασσός, 2nd ser., 12:253–61.

———. 1997. "Ἡ επιστημονική έρευνα γύρω από τον Καισάριο Δαπόντε." Αρχείο Πεπαρηθιακών Μελετών 1:41–46.

Tolias, George. 2010. "Maps Printed in Greek during the Age of Enlightenment, 1665–1820." e-Perimetron 5:1–48. http://www.e-perimetron.org/Vol_5_1/htm.

Tselikas, Agamemnon. 2004. Τα κατά και μετά την εξορίαν επισυμβάντα. By Callinicus III, Patriarch of Constantinople. Athens: Μορφωτικό Ἴδρυμα Εθνικής Τραπέζης.

Vagenas, Nasos. 1994. "Καισάριος Δαπόντες." In Ἡ εἰρωνικὴ γλῶσσα: Κριτικὲς μελέτες γιὰ τὴ νεοελληνικὴ γραμματεία, 172–76. Athens: Στιγμή.

———. 2013. "Μια μακρινή επέτειος." In Σημειώσεις από την αρχή του αιώνα, 336–40. Athens: Πόλις.

Veis, Nikolaos A. 1942. "Τὰ 'Ἄνθη νοητὰ' τοῦ Κωνσταντίνου-Καισαρίου Δαπόντε καὶ τὰ μοναστήρια τῆς Πελοποννήσου." Νέα Ἑστία, no. 373 (Χριστούγεννα 1942): 13–23.

Vivilakis, Iosif. 2013. Τὸ κήρυγμα ὡς performance: Ἐκκλησιαστικὴ ῥητορικὴ καὶ θεατρικὴ τέχνη μετὰ τὸ Βυζάντιο. Athens: Ἁρμός.

[Voulgaris, Eugenios]. 1768. "Περὶ τῶν διχονοιῶν τῶν ἐν ταῖς ἐκκλησίαις τῆς Πολωνίας: Δοκίμιον ἱστορικὸν καὶ κριτικὸν" ἐκ τῆς γαλλικῆς . . . μεταφρασθὲν μετὰ καὶ σημειωμάτων τινῶν ἱστορικῶν καὶ κριτικῶν, οἷς ἐν τέλει προσετέθη καὶ Σχεδίασμα περὶ τῆς ἀνεξιθρησκείας. [Leipzig].

Ware, Kallistos. 1995. The Orthodox Way. Rev. ed. Crestwood, NY: St. Vladimir's Seminary Press.

———. 2005. "St. Nikodimos and the Philokalia." In Mount Athos, the Sacred Bridge: The Spirituality of the Holy Mountain, edited by Dimitri Conomos and Graham Speake, 69–121. Oxford: Peter Lang.

Xeropotaminos, Zacharias. 2012. *Συμπληρωματικός κατάλογος ελληνικών χειρογράφων Ιεράς Μονής Ξηροποτάμου Αγίου Όρους (426–557)*. Thessalonike: Κέντρο Βυζαντινών Ερευνών Α.Π.Θ.

———. 2013/14. "Καισαρίου Δαπόντε, Περί της ημετέρας σεβάσμιας και βασιλικής Μονής του Ξηροποτάμου, παρά τινών κτητόρων εκτίσθη, και μία σημείωση: δύο κείμενα που πρέπει να αποδοθούν στον συντάκτη τους." *Βυζαντινά* 33: 387–421

Zallony, Mark Philip. 1826. *An Essay on the Fanariotes*.... Translated by the Rev. Charles Swan. In *Journal of a Voyage up the Mediterranean* . . . , by the Rev. Charles Swan, 2:271–423. London: C. and J. Rivington. Originally published as *Essai sur les Fanariotes*... (Marseille: Antoine Ricard, 1824).

Works by Konstantinos Dapontes

~

This is a chronological list of works by Dapontes, ordered by the year of composition, except in the case of works published in Dapontes's lifetime, which are entered according to the year of publication. Unpublished works whose date of composition is unknown appear at the end. The list is far from complete, with scores of manuscripts containing writings by Dapontes held in libraries and monasteries in Greece and elsewhere. For further details about these manuscripts, see Legrand 1880–88, vol. 3; Soulogiannis 1997: 42–43; Galitis 1975; Gounaridis 1993; Xeropotaminos 2012 and 2013/14; and Karanasios 2016. This list does not include writings that were not intended for publication, such as letters and personal notes. Transcriptions of these have appeared in Legrand 1880–88, 1: τνε′–υμγ′, 3: lxxxii–lxxxiii; Deligiannis 1936; 1937; Kallianos 1987; Kadas 1988; and Patapios Kausokalyvitis 2008: 460–70. This list excludes works whose authorship has been contested (see Paizi-Apostolopoulou 2004).

1736 *Βιβλίον περιέχον τὰς ἱερὰς ἀκολουθίας τοῦ ἁγίου ἱερομάρτυρος Χαραλάμπους τοῦ θαυματουργοῦ, τῆς ὁσίας Ματρώνης τῆς Χιοπολίτιδος, τοῦ ἐν ἁγίοις πατρός ἡμῶν Σπυρίδωνος ἐπισκόπου Τριμυθοῦντος τοῦ θαυματουργοῦ . . . , ἐπιμελείᾳ καὶ διορθώσει Κωνσταντίνου Δαπόντε ἀναγνώστου, τοῦ ἐκ νήσου Σκοπέλου* (Bucharest, 1736).*

1743   Δακικαὶ ἐφημερίδες· ἤτοι, συμβεβηκότα τετραετοῦς μάχης Ὀθωμανορρώσσων πρός δε καὶ Ἀουστριακῶν μέχρις ἔτους 1739, συλλεχθέντα ἀπό τε πρωτοτύπων γραμμάτων καὶ αὐτοπτῶν αὐλικῶν τῆς ἡγεμονίας Οὐγγροβλαχίας, αὐθεντεύοντος Ἰωάννου Κωνσταντίνου Νικολάου βοεβόδα τοῦ Μαυροκορδάτου, παρὰ Κωνσταντίνου Δαπόντε τοῦ ἐκ νήσου Σκοπέλου, δευτέρου γραμματικοῦ τῆς αὐτοῦ Ὑψηλότητος καὶ κονσούλου τῶν Ἰγγλέζων.

Published in Legrand 1880–88, vol. 1.

1746   Βίβλος ἱερὰ περιέχουσα τὴν ἅπασαν ἀκολουθίαν τοῦ ἁγίου ἱερομάρτυρος Ῥηγίνου ἐπισκόπου Σκοπέλων, τὸν ἀκάθιστον ὕμνον εἰς τὸν τίμιον καὶ ζωοποιὸν σταυρὸν τοῦ Σωτῆρος ἡμῶν Χριστοῦ, μετάφρασιν διὰ στίχων πολιτικῶν εἰς τὸν λόγον περὶ ἐξόδου ψυχῆς καὶ τῆς δευτέρας παρουσίας, μετὰ προσθήκης διαλόγων δύο κατὰ ἀλφάβητον, νῦν πρῶτον τυπωθεῖσα ἀναλώμασι τοῦ τιμιωτάτου καὶ ἐλλογιμωτάτου ἐν ἄρχουσι μεγάλου γραμματικοῦ κυρίου Κωνσταντίνου Δαπόντε τοῦ ἐκ νήσου Σκοπέλων (Venice: Francesco Pitteri, 1746).

1758   "Ἐξήγησις τῆς θείας λειτουργίας ἀνελλειπής, καὶ λεπτομερής, συλλεχθεῖσα καὶ στιχουργηθεῖσα παρὰ Κωνσταντίνου Δαπόντε, τοῦ μετονομασθέντος Καισαρίου."

For details about this manuscript, see Paizi-Apostolopoulou 2007b, 145–62. The work was published posthumously as Ἐξήγησις τῆς θείας λειτουργίας, συλλεχθεῖσα καὶ στιχουργηθεῖσα παρὰ Κωνσταντίνου Δαπόντε, τοῦ μετονομασθέντος Καισαρίου, vol. 1 (Vienna: Μαρκίδες Πούλιου, 1795).

1763   Λόγος τοῦ ἐν ἁγίοις πατρός ἡμῶν Κυρίλλου ἀρχιεπισκόπου Ἀλεξανδρείας περὶ ἐξόδου ψυχῆς καὶ περὶ τῆς δευτέρας παρουσίας τοῦ Κυρίου ἡμῶν Ἰησοῦ Χριστοῦ, μεταφρασθεὶς εἰς ἁπλῆν διάλεκτον διὰ στίχων πολιτικῶν παρὰ κυρίου Κωνσταντίνου Δαπόντε... (Venice: Δημήτριος Θεοδοσίου, 1763).

1764   "Φανάρι γυναικῶν· τουτέστι, βιβλίον φανερῶνον ἀρχαίων γυναικῶν ἐθνικῶν τε καὶ χριστιανῶν ἱστορίας θαυμασίας."

The preface of this work is published in Soulogiannis 1970, 257–60. Two dramatic dialogues from this manuscript are published in Vivilakis 2013, 475–86.

1766   *Καθρέπτης γυναικῶν ..., ἐν ᾧ φαίνονται γραφικῶς αἱ ἐν τῇ Παλαιᾷ Γραφῇ περιεχόμεναι σποράδην ἱστορίαι κακῶν τε καὶ καλῶν γυναικῶν, συντεθεῖσαι μὲν καὶ στιχουργηθεῖσαι παρὰ Κωνσταντίνου Δαπόντε, τοῦ μετονομασθέντος Καισαρίου,* 2 vols. (Leipzig: Breitkopf, 1766).

Two stories from vol. 1 ("Η θυσία του Ιεφθάε" and "Ιστορία Σωσάννης") are published in Savvidis 1993. A smaller selection appears in Savvidis 1995a, 273–306.

1768   "Ἄνθη νοητά· τουτέστι, βιβλίον περιέχον ἀνθολογίαν τῆς Παλαιᾶς Γραφῆς, καὶ διαλόγους, καὶ λόγους τινάς, καὶ ἄλλα διάφορα...."

Extracts of this manuscript have been published in Papadop[o]ulos-Kerameus 1909.

1768   *Κῆπος χαρίτων· τουτέστι, βιβλίον περιέχον τὴν περίοδον τοῦ τιμίου ξύλου τοῦ ζωοποιοῦ σταυροῦ, τοῦ ἐν τῇ ἱερᾷ καὶ βασιλικῇ Μονῇ τοῦ Ξηροποτάμου, τῇ οὔσῃ ἐν τῷ ἁγιωνύμῳ Ὄρει τοῦ Ἄθωνος, καὶ ἄλλα διάφορα....*

This work has been published several times: Sophokles 1880 (with some omissions; noted in Savvidis 1995a: 421); Legrand 1881: 1–232; Savvidis 1995a; Angelou 1997.

ca. 1770–74   "Βίβλος βασιλειῶν."

A short extract from this unpublished work appears in Savvidis 1991a: 42–44. See also Legrand 1880–88, 3:lxxxi–lxxxii; and Kechagioglou 2009.

1770   Ἐγκόλπιον λογικόν· τουτέστιν, ὕμνοι εἰς τὴν πανύμνητον
        Θεοτόκον, καὶ εὐχαὶ διὰ στίχων διαφόρων μετρῶν τε καὶ
        μελῶν, ποιηθέντες εἰς ὠφέλειαν καὶ χαρὰν τῶν μετ᾽ εὐλαβείας
        ἀναγινωσκόντων παρὰ τοῦ ταπεινοῦ Κωνσταντίνου Δαπόντε, τοῦ
        μετονομασθέντος Καισαρίου (Venice: Antonio Bortoli, 1770).

1770   Χρηστοήθεια, περιέχουσα καὶ διδάσκουσα τοὺς τρόπους δι᾽ ὧν
        ἀποκτῶνται τὰ καλὰ καὶ εὔτακτα ἤθη τῆς ψυχῆς καὶ τοῦ
        σώματος, μετὰ προσθήκης λόγων τινῶν, καὶ ἱστοριῶν, καὶ
        ὕμνων, μεταφρασθεῖσα καὶ στιχουργηθεῖσα παρὰ Κωνσταντίνου
        Δαπόντε, τοῦ μετανομασθέντος Καισαρίου (Venice: Δημήτριος
        Θεοδοσίου, 1770).

1776   Ἐπιστολαὶ διὰ στίχων ἁπλῶν κατὰ τῆς ὑπερηφανείας καὶ περὶ
        ματαιότητος κόσμου . . . (Venice: Antonio Bortoli, 1776).

        For an overview of the compositions contained in this volume, see
        Legrand 1880–88, 3: xlvi–xlvii. One of them, "Περὶ ματαιότητος
        κόσμου καὶ ἀθλιότητος τοῦ ἀνθρώπου," is translated here; it was
        published in Daoutis 1818: 40–56, and subsequently in Frantzi
        1993: 93–118.

1778   Τράπεζα πνευματικὴ Καισαρίου Δαπόντε· ἤτοι, βίβλος περιέχουσα
        ἱστορικούς, ἠθικοὺς καὶ ἐγκωμιαστικοὺς λόγους δεκαπέντε,
        συντεθέντας εἰς δόξαν Θεοῦ καὶ ὠφέλειαν τῶν ἀναγινωσκόντων
        (Venice: Νικόλαος Γλυκύς, 1778).

1778   Λόγοι πανηγυρικοί, εἰς ἁπλοῦς στίχους εἰς ἐγκώμιον διαφόρων
        ἁγίων (Venice: Δημήτριος Θεοδοσίου, 1778).

        Dapontes's "Κανὼν" ("Canon of Hymns") appears on pp. 107–16
        at the end of this work. The full title is: "Κανὼν περιεκτικὸς πολλῶν
        ἐξαιρέτων πραγμάτων τῶν εἰς πολλὰς πόλεις, καὶ νήσους, καὶ ἔθνη, καὶ
        ζῶα, ἐγνωσμένων." Details of its publication history can be found in
        Savvidis 1991a: 53–54. Dapontes's "Εἴδησις" ("Notice") appears at
        the end of the book (pp. 118–20).

1779   Μαργαρίται τῶν τριῶν Ἱεραρχῶν· ἤτοι, λόγοι παραινετικοὶ τῶν
        ἐν ἁγίοις πατέρων ἡμῶν καὶ οἰκουμενικῶν μεγάλων διδασκάλων,

Βασιλείου τοῦ Μεγάλου, Γρηγορίου τοῦ Θεολόγου, καὶ Ἰωάννου
τοῦ Χρυσοστόμου, μεταφρασθέντες εἰς τὸ ἁπλοῦν εἰς ὠφέλειαν
κοινὴν παρὰ Κωνσταντίνου Δαπόντε, τοῦ μετονομασθέντος
Καισαρίου (Venice: Νικόλαος Γλυκύς, 1779).

1780   Πατερικὸν τοῦ ἐν ἁγίοις πατρὸς ἡμῶν Γρηγορίου τοῦ Διαλόγου
πάπα Ῥώμης, ἐν ᾧ περιέχονται βίοι τῶν ἐν Ἰταλίᾳ ὁσίων πατέρων,
ὑπ᾽ αὐτοῦ μὲν λατινιστὶ συγγραφέντες, παρὰ δὲ τοῦ μακαρίου
Ζαχαρίου πάπα Ῥώμης εἰς τὸ ἑλληνικὸν μεταφρασθέντες, νῦν δὲ
εἰς τὸ κοινὸν παρὰ Κωνσταντίνου Δαπόντε τοῦ μετονομασθέντος
Καισαρίου, τοῦ ἐκ τῆς νήσου Σκοπέλων, πρὸς χρῆσιν κοινὴν καὶ
ὠφέλειαν τῶν ἀναγινωσκόντων (Venice: Νικόλαος Γλυκύς,
1780).

Selections from this volume appear in Savvidis 1995a: 331–419.

1781–82 "Γεωγραφικὴ ἱστορία· ἤγουν, βιβλίον περιέχον τὰς βασιλείας
καὶ αὐθεντείας, τὰς πόλεις καὶ νήσους τῶν τεσσάρων μερῶν
τῆς οἰκουμένης, Ἀσίας, Εὐρώπης, Ἀφρικῆς καὶ Ἀμερικῆς,
ἔτι δὲ λόγους πανηγυρικοὺς καὶ κανόνας, συντεθὲν καὶ τόδε
πρὸς τοῖς ἄλλοις εἰς δόξαν μὲν τοῦ ποιητοῦ τῶν ἀπάντων θεοῦ,
εἰς ὠφέλειαν δὲ καὶ μάθησιν, καὶ χαρὰν τῶν μετὰ χαρᾶς αὐτὸ
ἀναγινωσκόντων."

For a detailed description of the contents of this unpublished manu-
script, see Sathas 1872: ξε´–ξξ´. Extracts have been published in
Legrand 1881: 247–79; 1880–88, 3:lviii–lxxv; and Savvidis 1995a:
307–30.

1784   Κατάλογος ἱστορικὸς ἀξιόλογος τῶν καθ᾽ ἡμᾶς χρηματισάντων
ἐπισήμων Ῥωμαίων, καί τινων μεγάλων συμβεβηκότων καὶ
ὑποθέσεων, ἀρχόμενος ἀπὸ τοῦ χιλιοστοῦ ἑπτακοσιοστοῦ ἔτους
ἕως τοῦ ἐνεστῶτος ὀγδοηκοστοῦ τετάρτου, καταστρωθεὶς παρὰ
Κωνσταντίνου Δαπόντε Σκοπελίτου τοῦ μετονομασθέντος
Καισαρίου.

Published in Sathas 1872: 73–200, and Erbiceanu 1888: 87–227.

[?]   "Θέατρον βασιλικόν, ἐν ᾧ περιέχονται λόγοι πανηγυρικοὶ καὶ ὕμνοι Κωνσταντίνου Δαπόντε τοῦ μετονομασθέντος Καισαρίου."

Selections have been published in Legrand 1880–88, 3:lxxv–lxxx.

[?]   Ἐκλογὴ τῶν μετὰ τὴν ἅλωσιν Κωνσταντινουπόλεως νεοφανῶν μαρτύρων, τῶν ὑπὲρ τοῦ ὀνόματος τοῦ Χριστοῦ μαρτυρησάντων.

The manuscript has recently been published in Paschalides 2012.

TEXTS AND TRANSLATION

ΓΕΩΓΡΑΦΙΚΗ ΙΣΤΟΡΙΑ/
GEOGRAPHICAL HISTORY

"Γεωγραφικὴ ἱστορία"*

Εἰς δὲ τὸ Μπάμπι Χουμαγιοὺν, τούτέστι τὸ σαράγι,
εἰς τοῦτο μπῆκα δυὸ φοραὶς, καὶ εἶχαν μὲ ὑπάγη
εἰς τὸν ὀντᾶ, ὁποῦ ἐδῶ εἶναι πεφυλαγμένα
ὅπλα Ρωμαίων παλαιὰ, ἄρματα μαζωμένα.
Εἶναι δὲ 'ς τὸν ταραπχανᾶ αὐτός ἐκεῖ πλησίον,
ὁποῦ τὸ πλῆθος κόπτουσιν ἀσπρῶν, γροσῶν, φλωρίων·
καὶ κροκοδείλους εἶδα δυὸ, Νείλου κακὰ θηρία,
ταριχευτοὺς καὶ φοβεροὺς, τρόμος τῇ ἀληθείᾳ.
Μετὰ τοῦ Ἰωάνβοδα, αὐθέντου Μπογδανίας,
πρώτην φορὰν ἐμβήκαμεν μετ' ἀρχοντολογίας,
ὅστις ἐπροκαλέσθηκε τὴν κοῦκαν νὰ φορέσῃ,
τὴν τάξιν τὴν αὐθεντικὴν διὰ ν' ἀποτελέσῃ,
καὶ πρῶτα μὲν εἰσήλθομεν εἰς ἕνα τῶν ὀδάδων,
εἰς ὅν βεζίρης κάθηται μετὰ τῶν οὐλεμάδων·
ἦτον ἡμέρα τρίτη γὰρ καὶ καλαμπᾶ διβάνι,
καὶ προσκυνήσαντες εὐθὺς, βγήκαμεν 'ς τὸ μεϊντάνι·
τέσσαρες χιλιάδες δὲ ἐκοίτοντο πουγγία,
ἐκεῖ 'ς τὴν πόρτα τοῦ ὀδᾶ, ἔξωθεν, παρρησίᾳ·
ἦτον ψηλὰ δὲ 'ς τὸν ὀδᾶ καφάσι βεβαμμένο,
κ' ἕνα μανίκι εκ αυτού βελούδο κρεμασμένο,
μανίκι κόκκινο, πλατὺ, μακρὺ ὡς τρεῖς, λογιάζω,
πήχεις, 'ς τὴν στην κόγχην τοῦ ὀδᾶ, θαρρεῖς καὶ τὸ κυττάζω·
ὁ βασιλεὺς, λέγουν, ἐδῶ κάθηται, ἀκροᾶται
τὰς κρίσεις, πλὴν δὲν ὁμιλεῖ ποσῶς, οὐδὲ ὁρᾶται·
ἀφ' οὗ δὲ τὸ διβάνι τους τελείωσεν, ἐσώθη,
'ς τοὺς γιανιτζάρους ὁ λουφὲς ὁ τῶν πουγγιῶν ἐδόθη·
ἔπειτα μετὰ τὸν λουφὲ, εὐθύς ἐτραπεζώθη
τῶν γιανιτζάρων ὁ τζορβᾶς, καὶ κατὰ γῆς ἐστρώθη·
καὶ διὰ τὸν αὐθέντην δὲ τότε ἐτραπεζώθη
πλουσία τράπεζα, καλὴ, εἰς ὅλους μας ἐδόθη·
κ' εἰς τοὺς ἐλτζήδαις τὸ αὐτό γίνεται, ὅταν πάγουν
νὰ ἀνταμώσουν, καὶ αὐτοί ἐδῶ πρέπει να φάγουν.

* The passage is published in Legrand 1881: 247–49; it corresponds to F.98–F.99 of the original manuscript.

Extract from "Geographical History"

In the Bab-i-Humayun, the seraglio that is,
I entered twice and there they took me
To the room that holds a store of weapons
And the Byzantines' old armoury.
This place is situated near the mint
Where the mass of gold and silver coins are made.
I also saw a pair of taxidermic crocodiles
Those dreadful, fearsome creatures of the Nile.
The first occasion was with Prince Ioannes
And all high-ranking notables, when he
Was called to wear the ceremonial robe
To undertake the office of the prince.
We entered first one of the chambers
Where the vizier presides with the ulema.
It was a Tuesday, the divan was thronged;
We bowed at once then went out to the square.
Four thousand purses lay there in a pile
In full view, by the entrance of the chamber.
High up in the chamber was a coloured grille
From which there hung a wide, velvet drape,
A crimson-coloured drape, three cubits long,
I figure, in the corner of the room.
They say that here the Sultan sits and listens
To the councils, neither speaking nor appearing.
When their divan was over and dismissed,
The janissaries received their pay.
And after that they made the preparations
For the janissaries' soup, and laid it on the ground.
And for the prince and all of us
They then prepared a grand and lavish meal.
The same is offered to ambassadors.
When they visit, this is where they have to eat.

Μετὰ τὴν τράπεζαν εὐθὺς ὁ ἡγεμὼν ἐκλήθη·
τοῦ βασιλέως ἔμπροσθεν ἐβγῆκ᾽, ἐπαραστήθη,
παρόντος τοῦ βεζίρ᾽ ὀρθοῦ, καὶ τοῦ τῆς βασιλείας
μεγάλου δραγομάνου τε χάριν διερμηνείας,
καὶ μὲ καφτὰν βασιλικὸ καὶ κοῦκα φορεμένος
ἐβγῆκεν ὡς Μπογδάνμπεης, καὶ φιλοτιμημένος
ἕν ἄλογο βασιλικὸ χρυσοχαλινωμένο
καὶ μὲ τοποῦζ (ὄχι σπαθὶ) καὶ μόνον στολισμένο·
καβαλλικεύσας κίνησε, καὶ ἦλθε ᾽ς τὸ Φανάρι,
εἰς τὸ σεράγιον αὐτοῦ μ᾽ ἕνα πολὺ καμάρι,
μεχτερχανὲ βασιλικὸν, καὶ μὲ τῶν γιανιτζάρων
ἕναν ὀρτᾶ ὅλον πεζὸν, καὶ ὄχι καβαλλάρων,
καὶ μὲ ἡμᾶς ὡς εἴκοσι ὅλους καφτανωμένους,
τοὺς ἄρχοντάς του δηλαδὴ, ἀλογοκαθημένους.

After the repast the prince was called at once;
He came and stood before the Sultan
In the presence of the vizier
And Dragoman, the chief interpreter,
He donned the imperial caftan and the crest,
Emerging thus as prince of Moldavia
Honored with a royal, golden-bridled horse,
Decked only with a club (but not a sword).
Mounting the horse, to Phanari he came
Arriving at his mansion full of pride,
With a royal military band,
A janissary corps, all infantry,
And all of us, his twenty caftan-bearing
Notables, mounted each on horseback.

ΚΑΘΡΕΠΤΗΣ ΓΥΝΑΙΚΩΝ/ MIRROR OF WOMEN

Ἱστορία Σωσάννης*

Εἰς τῶν Ἑβραίων τὴν φυλὴν, τὴν τότ' εὐλογημένην,
Τώρα καταραμένην δὲ καὶ θεομισημένην,
Ἦτον, καὶ ἔλαμπε πολλὰ, καὶ εἰς τὴν εὐμορφίαν,
Ἀλλὰ καὶ εἰς τὴν γνῶσιν δὲ, καὶ εἰς τὴν ἀρχοντίαν,
Τούτη ἡ περιβόητος καὶ ἡ ἐξακουσμένη
Γυναῖκα, ὅσον εὔμορφη, τόσον καὶ τιμημένη.
Τιμὴ καὶ κλέος τῆς φυλῆς ἐκείνης τῶν Ἑβραίων,
Καὶ τοῦ ἀνδρός της καύχημα, καὶ δόξα τῶν γονέων,
Οἵτινες τὴν ἐδίδαξαν, ὡς δίκαιοι, τὸν νόμον,
Ἀπὸ μικρὴν τὴν ἔβαλαν εἰς τοῦ Θεοῦ τὸν δρόμον.
Καὶ διὰ τοῦτο τὸν Θεὸν πάντοτε ἐφοβεῖτο,
Ἐφύλαττε τὸν νόμον του, καὶ τὸν ἐσυλλογεῖτο.

. . . .

Ὁ δὲ ἄνδρας της ἤτονε ἕνας πολλὰ μεγάλος,
Πλούσιος, πολυκτήμωνας, ὥσπερ οὐδείς τις ἄλλος,
Καὶ εἶχεν εἰς τὸ σπῆτι του καὶ ἕνα περιβόλι,
Μεγάλον δὲ καὶ θαυμαστὸν, ποῦ ἐθαύμαζον ὅλοι.
Καὶ εἰς αὐτὸν ἐπήγαιναν ὅλοι οἱ Ἰουδαῖοι,
Κ' ἐκοίταζαν ταῖς κρίσες των, νέοι καὶ γηραλαῖοι,
Μὲ τὸ νὰ ἤτονε αὐτὸς ὁ πλέον τιμημένος,
Ὁ πάντων ενδοξότερος, καὶ πλέον στοχασμένος.
Ἐκείνην ὅμως τὴν χρονιά, εἶχαν διορισθῶσι
Δύο πρεσβύτεροι κριταὶ ὅλους νὰ κυβερνῶσι.
Ἐπήγαιναν στὸ σπῆτι του, λοιπόν, κ' ἐκαρτεροῦσαν,
Κ' ἐκεῖ ταῖς κρίσες τοῦ λαοῦ, ἔκαναν, θεωροῦσαν.
Καὶ ὅλοι ὅσοι εἴχασι διαφορὰν καμμίαν,
Ἤρχοντο εἰς τοὺς γέροντας μὲ κάθ' ἐλευθερίαν.
Καὶ ἤτονε το σπῆτι του ἀπ' τὸ πουρνὸ γεμάτο,

---

* The extracts are based on the first edition (1766) of *Καθρέπτης γυναικῶν* (1:99–131). I have
made minor alterations to the original text (capitalization, word separation, accents) and made
some adjustments in punctuation marks (including speech marks) to clarify meaning. No
changes have been made to the spelling of words.

Susanna

Among the Hebrew race, which once was blessed
But now is godforsaken and accursed,
There was a woman, dazzling in beauty
But in knowledge and in dignity as well;
A woman widely known and much esteemed,
Whose beauty was as great as her respect.
She was the fame and honor of that race,
Her husband's pride, and glory of her parents,
Righteous people who taught her the law
And from a young age set her on the path of God.
And so the Lord at all times did she fear,
Observing and considering his law.
. . . .
Her husband was a great and wealthy man
With grand possessions no one else could match.
And in his house he also had a garden,
A large and glorious one that everyone admired.
The Jewish people all, both young and old,
Would go to him to settle their disputes,
For he was very honorable,
The most discerning and esteemed of all.
But that year, two elders were appointed
As judges who would govern over all.
They frequented his house and waited there
To hear and try the cases of the people.
Whoever had a matter of dispute,
Came to the elders of their own accord.
The house was crowded from the morning

Ἕως τὴν ὥραν τοῦ φαγιοῦ, ὅλο ἀπάνω κάτω.
Ἀφ' οὗ δὲ πλέον εὔγαιναν κ' ἐπήγαινε καθένας,
Στὸ σπῆτι του, καὶ ἄνθρωπος δὲν ἔμενε κανένας,
Καὶ τότε ἔυγαινεν αὐτὴ, κ' εὐθὺς στὸ περιβόλι
Ἔμβαινε κ' ἐσεργιάνιζεν, ἄς μὴν ἦτον καὶ σχόλη.

Ἐκεῖνοι καὶ τὴν ἔβλεπαν αὐτὴν κάθε ἡμέραν,
Οἱ δύο μαῦροι κόρακες τὴν ἄσπρην περιστέραν,
Ὁποῦ στὸ περιβόλι της μπαίνουσα περπατοῦσε,
Καὶ πότ' ἐδὼ, πότε ἐκεῖ, πήγαινε κ' ἐθωροῦσε.

Καὶ πότε τριαντάφυλλα ἔκοπτε νὰ μυρίση,
Πότε καὶ ποῦ ἐστέκουνταν κ' ἔβλεπε κυπαρίσσι,
Κ' ἐχαίρουνταν στὸ ὕψος του καὶ στὴν πολλὴν ἰσιάδα,
Τοῦ τρανταφυλλιοῦ τὴν βαφήν, πάλιν, καὶ εὐμορφάδα.

Καὶ ὅταν στὴν τρανταφυλλιὰν ἐπήγαινε νὰ πιάση
Κανένα τριαντάφυλλον, κ' ἐχάνουνταν νὰ φθάση,
Ἐτότε δὲν ξεχώριζα, ἀληθινὰ σὲ κρίνω,
Ἀπὸ τὰ τριαντάφυλλα τὸ πρόσωπον ἐκεῖνο.

Πότε κλωνὶ βασιλικοῦ, πότε κανένα κρίνο,
Ἔσκυπτε τὸ βασιλικὸν κορμάκι της ἐκεῖνο
Κ' ἔκοπτε καὶ ἐμύριζε, καθὼς τὸ συνειθοῦσι
Ὅσοι στὰ περιβόλια, ἄνδρες γυναῖκες, μποῦσι.
Πολλάκις ἐτανύζετο γιὰ νὰ μπορῇ νὰ φθάση,
Κανένα ρόδι εὔμορφον, ἤ μῆλον, νὰ πιάση.

Καὶ ἐστοχάζουμουν αὐτὰ, κ' ἐκοίταζα κ' ἐκείνην,
Καὶ τὰ ἐσύγκρινα μαζί, μὰ μὲ δικαιοσύνην,
Κ' ἔβλεπα πῶς τὰ ξαπερνᾷ πολλὰ στὴν εὐμορφίαν
Ἡ εὔμορφη Σωσάννα μου, καὶ εἰς τὴν θεωρίαν.

Τὴν ἔβλεπα, κ' ἐχαίρουμουν, στὸ περιβόλιόν της,
Τὴν Εὔαν θάρρουν κ' ἔβλεπα, εἰς τὸν παράδεισόν της.
Ἐκεῖνοι τὴν ἐκοίταζαν, καὶ ἔκαμναν στὰ μάτια,
Κ' ἐγίνουνταν καὶ ἡ καρδιὰ τοῦ κάθ' ἑνὸς κομμάτια.
Καὶ ὡς καθὼς ἐκοίταξε διὰ νὰ ἀπατήση,
Ὁ ὄφις τὴν Προμήτορα, καὶ νὰ τὴν ἀτιμήση,
Ἐνέδρευον ὡς λέοντες, πότε νὰ τὴν ἁρπάσουν,

Up until the time for lunch, on every floor.
And after everyone had come and gone
And not a soul was left inside the house,
She would emerge and go straight to the garden
For a stroll, even if it were not a day of rest.
Every day the elders used to watch her
Like two black crows around a snowy dove,
As she made her way into the garden,
Walking and looking around here and there.
At times she picked a rose to smell,
At times she paused to view a cypress tree,
Rejoicing in its height and ample shade
Or in the hue and beauty of the rose.
And when she walked toward the rosebush
And, reaching for a rose, went out of sight,
In truth I say I could not tell apart
Her countenance amid the roses.
She lowered her stately figure,
For a sprig of basil here or lily there
To pick and smell, as men and women
Are wont to do when entering a garden.
She often reached out so she could get
A dainty pomegranate or touch an apple.
I contemplated these and looked at her,
And I compared them evenhandedly
And saw that my beautiful Susanna far
Outshone them in appearance and allure.
I rejoiced as I beheld her in her garden;
I felt I was beholding Eve in paradise.
The elders gaped at her with staring eyes,
The heart of each man breaking into pieces.
And like the serpent that did look on Eve
In order to deceive her and disgrace her,
Like lions they lay in wait to grab

Νὰ καταφάγουν τὴν πτωχὴν ὅλην καὶ νὰ χορτάσουν.
Ἐκηλαδοῦσαν τὰ πουλιά, κ' ἔστεκε κὶ ἀκροᾶτο,
Ἄφοβα, ὁλομόναχη, καὶ ποῖον ἐφοβᾶτο;
Καὶ πότ' ἐνοστιμεύουνταν τὴν λαλιὰν τοῦ σπείνου,
Καὶ πότε τούτου τοῦ πουλιοῦ, καὶ πάλιν πότ' ἐκείνου—
Τῆς καρδερίνας, τοῦ σκαθιοῦ, τοῦ κανναριοῦ δὲ πάλιν,
Λαλιὰν τὴν γλυκόστροφον, παρὰ καμμίαν ἄλλην,
Τὸ σφύρισμα τοῦ κόσσυφα, τὸ μουσικὸν ἐκεῖνο,
Ἀηδόνια, χελιδόνια, ἐτοῦτα τὰ ἀφίνω.
Πολλαῖς φοραῖς ἐστάθηκε, κ' ἔνιωσα νὰ τῆς δίδη
Πολλὴν γλυκύτητα φωνὴ ἡ τοῦ τρυποκαρίδι.
Ὅπου καλὸς καὶ δροσερὸς ἴσκιος νὰ καθήση,
Ὅπου καλὸς καὶ χλοερὸς τόπος νὰ σεργιανίση,
Κὶ ἀγάλι' ἀγάλια καὶ αὐτὴ τὰ χείλη νὰ κινήση,
Καὶ νὰ ἀνοίξ' τὸ στόμα της, ἐκεῖ νὰ τραγουδίση,
Κανένα στίχον νὰ εἰπῇ, ὅλο τιμὴ κ' ἐκεῖνος.
Ὅμως μὲ μίαν της φωνὴν, ἄλλο παρὰ σειρῆνος,
Πολλαῖς φοραῖς μὲ ἤρχετο στὸν νοῦν ὁ Κουκουζέλης,
Καὶ ὁ παμπάλαιος Ὀρφεὺς—τί ἄλλο πλέον θέλεις;
Θυμοῦμαι, ὥρα της καλὴ, καὶ δύο της κοτζάκια,
Ὁποῦ τὰ εἶπε, κάθοντας, ἐκεῖ στὰ χορταράκια:
«Ὢ τί καλὸν, καὶ τί τερπνὸν, εἶναι εἰς τοὺς ἀνθρώπους,
Νὰ κατοικοῦν παντοτινὰ, εἰσὲ τοιούτους τόπους!»
Ἀπ' ὅλους δὲ τοὺς ἴσκιους, τοῦ πεύκου ἀγαπούσε,
Ἐκεῖ συχνὰ ἐκάθητο καὶ κάμποσον ἀργοῦσε,
Ἐνοστιμεύουνταν πολλὰ τὸν ἴσκιον τὸν πολύν του,
Κ' ἐκεῖνον τὸν ξεχωριστὸν τὸν ἦχον τὸν γλυκύν του.
Ἐκεῖ μυρτιαῖς, κουκουναριαῖς—τὰ ἥμερα τ' ἀφίνω,
Διότι ἤτον περισσὰ στὸ περιβόλ' ἐκεῖνο.
Καὶ πότε μύρτην ἔπερνε καὶ τόβανε στὸ στόμα,
Πότε κανένα λούλουδον καὶ ἄλλο τι ἀκόμα.
Καὶ τό 'βανε στὸ στόμα της, καὶ στόμα δακτυλίδι,
Μὲ χείλη σὰν ρουμπίνια, πόσην στολὴν τῆς δίδει.
Ἴδια σὰν ἡ μέλισσα, ἔτζι ἀνθολογοῦσε

And wolf her down, poor thing, and have their fill.
She stood and listened to the chirping birds,
Alone and unafraid—for whom was there to fear?
She relished now the twitter of the finch,
The song of one bird here and another there—
The goldfinch and the siskin and canary,
Sweet-sounding in their song, beyond compare;
The tuneful warble of the blackbird,
Not to mention nightingales and swallows.
Many times she paused and I felt the chirping
Of the woodpecker added to her sweetness.
She took a seat where the shade was fine and cool,
A stroll where the path was fine and leafy,
And slowly she would start to part her lips,
Opening her mouth to raise her voice in song,
And sing a verse or two, most dignified.
Though she was no siren, one sound from her
Would often bring to mind Koukouzelis
And Orpheus of old—what more could one desire?
I recall a couplet, bless her,
Which she sang as she sat upon the turf:
"How pleasing, how delightful for mankind,
To always live in places such as these!"
Of all the shades, she loved the pine tree's most
And often sat there spending much time
Appreciating its abundant shade,
As well as its distinct and gentle sound.
Myrtles and pines were there—not to mention
Fruit trees, which were countless in that garden.
At times she picked and put a berry in her mouth,
At times a flower and something else besides.
She put it in her mouth—a ring-like mouth
With ruby lips bestowing on her much grace.
Just like a bee, she picked and plucked among

Ἀπὸ τὰ ἄνθη καὶ καρποὺς, μόνον πῶς δὲν πετοῦσε.
Και κυτριαῖς δὲν τὸ ἔλειπαν, ὄντας πολλὰ μεγάλο
Τὸ περιβόλι της αὐτὸ, καὶ κάθε ξύλο ἄλλο.
....
Καὶ φλαμουργιαῖς τρεῖς τέσσαρες, καὶ ὅλο εὐωδία
Ἦτον τὸ περιβόλιον, ὅλο τῇ ἀληθείᾳ,
Σχῖνοι δὲ ὅσους ἤθελες, ὁμοίως δὲ καὶ πρῖνοι.
Καὶ τοῦτα ὅλα μοναχὴ τὰ χαίρουνταν ἐκείνη.
Τὴν ἔβλεπα, κ᾽ ἐχαίρουμουν κ᾽ ἐγὼ ἐπ᾽ ἀληθείας,
Καὶ τὴν ἐκαλοτύχιζα, ἐκ βάθους τῆς καρδίας.
Οἱ γέροντες τὴν κοίταζαν κ᾽ ἔτριζαν τοὺς ὀδόντας,
Ἀπὸ μακριὰν τὴν ἔτρωγαν, στέκωντας καὶ θωρῶντας.
Τὸν νοῦν τους ἐδιάστρεψαν, ἐξέχασαν τὸν νόμον,
Δικαιοσύνης ἄφηκαν καὶ κρίσεως τὸν δρόμον.
Ἐγύρισαν τὰ μάτια τους, διὰ νὰ μὴ θωροῦσι
Ἀπάνω εἰς τὸν οὐρανὸν, καὶ φοβηθοῦν, συρθοῦσι.
Καὶ ἦσαν καὶ οἱ δύο τους ἐτοῦτοι κεντημένοι
Εἰς τὴν καρδίαν διὰ αὐτὴν, ἐρωτοπληγωμένοι.
Κἰ ὅμως δὲν ἐφανέρωσαν ἀλλήλους τους τὸν πόνον,
Μᾶλλον εἰπεῖν δὲ τὸν ψυχρὸν καὶ τὸν κακόν τους χρόνον.
Γιατὶ ἐντρέπωντο αὐτοὶ, διὰ νὰ ἐξηγήσουν
Φεῦ! τὴν ἐπιθυμίαν τους, νὰ τὴν κοινολογήσουν.
Μόνον ἐφύλαττον πολλὰ καὶ ἐπαρατηροῦσαν
Καὶ κάθε μέρα καὶ οἱ δυὸ ἐκείνην ἐθωροῦσαν,
Μὲ ἕνα πόνον καὶ οἱ δυὸ, μὲ μιὰν ἐπιθυμίαν,
Καὶ μὲ καρδίαν καὶ ψυχὴν τῶν δύο παρομοίαν.
Μίαν ἡμέραν εἴπασιν, ἀλλήλους των: «Ἄς πᾶμε,
Διότι εἶναι καὶ καιρὸς, στὰ σπήτια μας νὰ φᾶμε.»
Καὶ ἔτζι ἐχωρίσθηκαν ἕνας ἀπὸ τὸν ἄλλον,
Καὶ πάλιν ἐπιστρέψαντες, ὤ τῶν γουρνοκεφάλων!
Ἦλθασιν ἐπὶ τὸ αὐτὸ καὶ εἶχαν σμίξῃ πάλιν,
Ὁ ἕνας ἀπ᾽ τὴν μιὰ μεριὰ, κἰ ὁ ἄλλος ἀπ᾽ τὴν ἄλλην.
Ὁ ἕνας ἀπὸ τὴν ὀργὴν, κἰ ἄλλος ἀπ᾽ τὴν κατάρα,
Ἀπ᾽ τὸ ἀνάθεμα κ᾽ οἱ δυὸ, μὲ τὴν αὐτὴν λαχτάρα.

The flowers and fruit, though she did not have wings.
There was no lack of citron trees, so large
A grove it was, or any other tree.
. . . .
The linden trees were three or four, and full
Of fragrance was the orchard, truly so,
With mastic trees and oak trees in abundance.
And all of these she reveled in alone.
I looked at her and truly felt delight
And blessed her from the bottom of my heart.
The elders gazed at her and gnashed their teeth,
And stood feasting on her from afar.
Perverting their minds, they forgot the law
And left the course of justice and discernment.
They turned away their eyes, lest they should look
Up to Heaven, be frightened, and be swayed.
And both these men were smitten in their
Hearts with her, and overwhelmed with lust.
But they did not tell one another their distress,
Or one should say, their cold and evil thoughts.
For they were too ashamed to manifest
(Alas!) their passion and reveal it.
They only kept an eye on her and watched,
Both men espying her each and every day,
Both with the same distress and same desire,
Two elders both alike in heart and soul.
One day, they said to one another:
"Let us go back home, for it is time to eat."
And so they parted from each other,
But then they turned around again! What pigs!
They came to the same place and met again,
Each coming from a different direction.
One was filled with wrath, the other curses,
Both with blasphemy and with the same desire.

Καὶ ἐξετάζοντες εὐθὺς ἀλλήλους, τὴν αἰτίαν
Εἶπαν, καὶ ὡμολόγησαν πλιὸ τὴν ἐπιθυμίαν.
Καὶ ἔτζι ἐσυμφώνησαν νὰ ἐπιμεληθῶσι,
Μαζὶ νὰ εὕρουνε καιρὸν, μονάχην νὰ τὴν βρῶσι.

....

Περὶ τῆς Σωσάννης οὔσης εἰς τὸ λουτρὸν, μπήκασι καὶ οἱ γέροντες
Παρατηροῦντες, τὸ λοιπὸν, νὰ δράξουσι καμμίαν
Ἡμέραν, καθὼς ἤθελαν, γιὰ τὴν ἐπιθυμίαν,
Καὶ τοῦτο ἐνιαζόμενοι κ' οἱ δύο ὅλο ἕνα,
Κοιτάζωντες μὲ τέσσερα μάτια, μὰ τυφλωμένα,
Εὐγῆκεν πάλιν ἡ καλὴ, πάγει στὸ περιβόλι,
Ὡς χθὲς, προχθὲς, καὶ πάντοτε, καθημερνὴ καὶ σχόλη.
Μὲ δύο της κορίτζια, διὰ τὴν συντροφίαν,
Καθὼς πάντα συνείθιζε, καὶ γιὰ συνομιλίαν.
Ἐκεῖ τῆς ἦλθεν ὄρεξις, εἶχεν ἐπιθυμήσῃ,
Εἰς τὸ λουτρόν της νὰ λουσθῇ, τὸ σῶμα νὰ δροσίσῃ.
Μία ἡμέρα ἔτυχε, τότε, πολλὰ καμένη,
Λουτρὸς καὶ εὐμορφώτατος, λοιπὸν τίς δὲν ἐμβαίνει;
Ἄνθρωπος καὶ δὲν φαίνεται, ψυχὴ στὸ περιβόλι,
Ποῦ 'ξευρε, πῶς εὑρίσκονται κρυμμένοι οἱ διαβόλοι;

....

Καὶ εἶπε τὰ κορίτζια: «Πηγαίνετε ὁμάδι,
Καὶ φέρετε τὰ λουτρικὰ, πάρετε καὶ τὸ λάδι.
Κλείσατε καὶ τὰς θύρας δὲ, καὶ γλήγορα να 'λθῆτε,
Διότι θέλω νὰ λουσθῶ, καὶ μὴν ἀργοπορῆτε.»
Εὐθὺς δὲ ὁποῦ βγήκασιν, ἐκείναις, καὶ τραβοῦσι
Ταῖς πόρταις τοῦ περιβολιοῦ, ὡς εἶπε, καὶ σφαλοῦσι,
Εὐθὺς συκώνονται αὐτοὶ, ὡσὰν δαιμονισμένοι,
Καὶ τρέχουσιν ἀπάνω της, σὰν σκύλοι λυσσασμένοι.
Ἔτρεξαν καὶ οἱ δύο τους, εἰς τὸ λουτρὸν ἐμπῆκαν,
Καὶ ὡς καθὼς τὴν ἤθελαν, ἀλήθια τὴν εὕρηκαν.
Ἔλιωσαν σὰν τὴν εἴδασι, τάραξεν ἡ καρδιά τους,
Ἔχασαν καὶ τὰ λόγια τους, καὶ τὰ συλλογικά τους.

They questioned one another, finally
Admitting to the reason and their lust.
And so they both agreed to come up with a plan,
To find a time when she would be alone.
. . . .

The elders enter while Susanna is in the pool
While they were waiting thus to chance upon
A day for their desire, as they so wished,
And both men thinking of this all the time,
Keeping watch with four, yet sightless, eyes,
Out she came again and went into the garden
As yesterday and every day of work and rest.
She went with two housemaids, as was her wont,
Who talked with her and kept her company.
There she had the urge, she had the wish
To bathe in the pool to cool her body down.
It happened to be burning hot that day.
The pool was most attractive—who would not go in?
No person was in sight, no soul around the grove,
How could she have known that demons lay in wait?
. . . .
She said to her maids: "Go back together
And fetch my bathing kit; bring too the oil.
Secure the doors and come back straightaway
For I desire to bathe; do not be late."
As soon as they had gone, and pulled and barred
The garden gates as she had told them to,
The elders rose, as if they were possessed,
And charged at her like rabid dogs.
The two men ran and went inside the pool,
And found her there exactly as they wished.
They melted at the sight; their heart did shake;
They lost the power of speech, their mind as well.

Ἀφ᾽ οὗ τὴν ἐψηλάφισαν μὲ τὰ ὀμμάτιά τους
Καὶ τὴν καλοστοχάσθηκαν κάμποσον ἀρκετά τους,
Χωρὶς νὰ τὴν ἐγγίξωσι, χωρὶς νὰ τὴν βιάσουν,
Ἢ νὰ βάλουν ἀπάνω της χέρι καὶ νὰ τὴν πιάσουν,
Ἀνοίγουσι τὸ στόμα τους, καὶ λέγουσι, μιλοῦσι,
Ὅσα τὸ πάθος κὶ ὁ καιρὸς τοὺς ἔδινε νὰ ποῦσι.
Τέλος, τὴν ἀπεφάσισαν ἕνα νὰ διαλέξῃ:
Τὸν θάνατον, ἢ τὴν ζωὴν ἔχει σκοπὸν νὰ στέρξῃ;
«Ἂν θέλῃς,» εἶπαν, «τὴν ζωὴν, κάμε τὴν ὄρεξίν μας.
Ἰδὲς πόσα ἐσύντρεξαν εἰς εὐχαρίστησίν μας:
Τόπος, καὶ τρόπος, καὶ καιρὸς, ἄδεια, μοναξία,
Κριταὶ οἱ παρακαλεσταὶ, καὶ πᾶσα εὐκολία.
Εἰ δὲ, νὰ ξεύρῃς βέβαια, πῶς θέλομεν εἰποῦμεν,
Μὲ ἕναν πῶς σὲ ηὕραμεν, καὶ σὲ λιθοβολοῦμεν.»
Ταῦτα ἀκούοντας ἐγὼ, καὶ βλέπωντας κ᾽ ἐκείνην,
Μὲ μίαν μου ἐλεεινὴν καὶ ἄκραν μου ὀδύνην,
Μὲ ἦλθε τότε εἰς τὸν νοῦν, ἐμένα τοῦ ἰδίου,
Ἐκείνη ἡ Βηρσαβεὲ, γυναῖκα τοῦ Οὐρίου.
. . . .

Λόγια Σωσάννης πρὸς αὑτοὺς
. . . .

Ταῦτα ἀκούσασα, λοιπὸν, στέναξεν ἐκ καρδίας,
Καὶ λέγει ἔτζι στοὺς κριτὰς τούτους τῆς ἀδικίας:
«Στενά μου εἶναι πάντοθεν. Ἂν κάμω ἁμαρτίαν,
Θάνατος εἶναι ψυχικὸς δίχως ἀμφιβολίαν.
Ἐὰν δὲν κάμω, πάλιν δὲ, τὰ χέρια τὰ δικά σας
Δὲν τὰ γλυτώνω, βέβαια, χέρια τὰ φονικά σας.
Προκρίνω δὲ καλήτερα, δίχως νὰ ἁμαρτήσω,
Νὰ πέσω εἰς τὰ χέρια σας, ν᾽ ἀδικοθανατήσω,
Παρὰ ἐνώπιον Θεοῦ ἐγὼ τώρα νὰ πταίσω,
Μὲ τὸ ἁμάρτημα αὐτὸ, στὰς χεῖρας Του νὰ πέσω.
Λέτε πῶς δὲν εἶναι κανεὶς ἐδὼ νὰ μᾶς κοιτάξῃ,
Νὰ μᾶς ἰδῇ τί κάμωμεν, καὶ τί θέλομεν πράξει.
Ἀμὴ δὲν εἶναι ὁ Θεός; Δὲν στέκει ἀοράτως

After they had probed her with their eyes
And contemplated her for quite some time,
Without defiling her or touching her,
Or laying a finger to take hold of her,
They opened their mouth and voiced whatever
The occasion and their passion made them say.
At last they decided that she should choose:
Is it life or death that she would rather have?
"If you want to live, submit to our desire.
See how much is working in our favor:
The place, the means, the time, the isolation,
The very ease, beseeching you as judges.
If you refuse, be sure that we will say
We found you with a man, and you'll be stoned."
 I heard these words myself, and as I looked at her
To my immense and pitiful distress,
The thought that came to my own mind
Was Bathsheba, the wife of Uriah.

. . . .

Susanna speaks to the elders

. . . .

She heard these words and gave a heartfelt sigh
And spoke thus to these judges of injustice:
"I am completely trapped. For if I sin,
It will, no doubt, bring on my spiritual death.
And yet, if I do not, I still cannot
Escape your hands, those lethal hands of yours.
I would sooner sinless be, fall into
Your hands and be unjustly put to death,
Than in the eyes of God commit offense
And with this sin fall in His hands instead.
You say that not a soul is here to see,
To witness our actions and our deeds.
But isn't God here, who stands invisibly,

Αὐτός ποῦ εἶναι πανταχοῦ, κὶ ὅλος μάτια γεμάτος;
Ἐγὼ δὲ περισσότερον τὸν Κύριον φοβοῦμαι,
Καὶ περισσότερον αὐτὸν τρέμω καὶ συλλογοῦμαι,
Παρὰ τὸν ἄνδρα μου αὐτὸν, καὶ συγγενεῖς, καὶ ἄλλους,
Ξένους ἀνθρώπους κ' ἐδικοὺς, μικρούς τε καὶ μεγάλους.
Νὰ μὴ τ' ὁρίσῃ ὁ Θεὸς ποτέ μου ἁμαρτίαν
Νὰ κάμω, ἤ νὰ φαντασθῶ μέσα εἰς τὴν καρδίαν.
Καὶ ἄν κακονοματισθῶ καὶ χάσω τὴν τιμήν μου,
Ἤ, τέλος, ἐξ αἰτίας σας, καὶ τούτην τὴν ζωήν μου,
Ὁ ἐπουράνιος Θεὸς, διὰ τὴν ἀδικίαν,
Θέλει μὲ δώσει τὴν ζωὴν, καὶ δόξαν αἰωνίαν.»
Ἐτοῦτα εἶπεν εἰς αὐτοὺς τὰ λόγια, ὡς τυχαίνει,
Ὄχι ὡς ἡ Βηρσαβεὲ, καὶ τούτ' ὑπανδρευμένη.
....
Καὶ ἐφώναξε παρευθὺς ἐκεῖ φωνὴν μεγάλην,
Ἐφώναξαν δὲ καὶ αὐτοὶ, ἀπ' τὴν μεριὰ τὴν ἄλλην.
Καὶ τρέχει ἕνας ἀπ' αὐτοὺς, καὶ τοῦ περιβολίου
Ταῖς πόρταις ἄνοιξεν εὐθὺς (ὦ στοχασμὸς τ' ἀχρείου!)
Ὡς ἤκουσαν δὲ τὴν φωνὴν, πηδοῦσι καὶ εὐγαίνουν,
Ὅλοι τοῦ ὁσπητίου της, στὸ περιβόλι μπαίνουν.
Καὶ ὡς, καθὼς ἀκούουσι, τὰ λόγια τῶν γερόντων,
Μεγάλως κατησχύνθηκε τὸ πλῆθος τῶν παρόντων.
Ὅτι ποτὲ λόγος κακὸς τοιοῦτος δὲν ἐρρέθη,
Περὶ αὐτῆς τῆς γυναικὸς, ἄμεμπτος γὰρ εὑρέθη.
Κλαίουσιν ἡ δουλεύτραις της, σχίζουν τὰ μάγουλά τους,
Οἱ δοῦλοι της ἐπάγωσαν, τρέμουν τὰ χέριά τους.
Ὥρα νὰ πῇς δὲν πέρασε, κ' εὐθὺς τρέχει ἡ φήμη
(Πάντα εἰς τέτοιαις δουλειαῖς αὐτὴ εἶναι ἑτοίμη)
Καὶ φέρνει καὶ τὸν ἄνδρα της, καὶ τοὺς γονεῖς ἀπόντας,
(Διότι, τοῦτο ἔγινε, σπῆτι αὐτὸς μὴν ὄντας).
....
Τόσος, λοιπὸν, κόσμος, λαὸς, ἦλθεν, ἐσυμμαζεύθη
Στὸ σπῆτι τοῦ Ἰωακεὶμ, ἀφ' οὗ ἐμαθητεύθη.
Μῆλον νὰ ἔρριχνες ἐκεῖ, ὡς λέγ' ἡ παροιμία,

Is ever present and all-seeing?
It is the Lord I fear the most, I dread
Him and abide by Him, more than my
Own husband, relatives and other people,
Be they strangers, friends, young ones or old.
May God ordain that I should never sin,
Let alone conceive it in my heart.
And if I should be slandered, lose my honor,
Or, because of you, forfeit my very life,
Heavenly God, in view of the injustice,
Will grant me glory and eternal life."
These are the words she spoke to them, unlike
Bathsheba, who was a married woman too.
. . . .

Thereupon, she cried out with a loud voice,
And from the other side they cried out too.
And one of them ran forth to open up
The garden gates (o what a cunning thought!)
When all the household heard the cry,
They gave a start and rushed into the garden.
And as they listened to the elders,
The crowd there present felt deeply ashamed.
For never had an evil word been said
About this woman, blameless as she was.
Her housemaids cried out loud and tore their cheeks,
Her servants stood in shock with trembling hands.
No time went by, the rumour quickly spread
—as rumours always do in times like these—
And fetched her absent husband and her parents
(For this had happened while he had been out).
. . . .

A multitude of people gathered round
At the house of Joakim, when news had spread.
An apple thrown there, as the saying goes,

Κάτω στὴν γῆν δὲν ἔπιπτεν, ὄχι τῇ ἀληθείᾳ.
Ἦλθασι καὶ προσμέvασι, μὲ τέσσαρα ἀφτία,
Ν᾽ ἀκούσουν τί ἀπόφασις βγαίνει ἀπ᾽ τὰ θηρία.

....

Τότε γυρίζουν, τὸ λοιπὸν, καὶ λέγουν ὁμοφώνως
Καὶ μὲ θυμὸν οἱ γέροντες, μὰ καὶ μεγαλοφώνως:
«Στείλετε, φέρετε ἐδὼ, τὴν κόρην τοῦ Χαλκίου,
Γυναῖκα τοῦ Ἰωακεὶμ, ἄρχοντος τοῦ τιμίου.»
Εὐθὺς τῆς ὥρας ἔστειλαν, καὶ ἦλθεν ἡ Σωσάννα,
Καὶ τὰ παιδία της μαζῖ, καὶ ὁ πατὴρ, κ᾽ ἡ μάνα,
Καὶ ὅλοι της οἱ συγγενεῖς καὶ οἱ οἰκειακοί της,
Ὁποῦ ἐμαζωχθήκασι, καὶ ἦτανε μαζί της.
Ἡ δὲ Σωσάννα ἤτονε πάρα πολλὰ ὡραία,
Καὶ παρὰ φύσιν εὔμορφη καὶ τρυφερὴ καὶ νέα.
Ὅθεν οἱ ἀσεβέστατοι, διὰ νὰ τὴν χορτάσουν,
Ὥρισαν, οἱ θεόργιστοι, νὰ τὴν ἐξεσκεπάσουν.

....

Ψευδομαρτυρία κατὰ Σωσάννης

....

Καὶ ἔτζι, μὲ τὰ χέρια ἀπάνω στὸ κεφάλι,
Ἀνοίγουσι τὸ μιαρὸν στόμα οἱ ταϊφάλοι,
Καὶ λέγουν εἰς ἐπήκοον πάντων καὶ παρρησίᾳ,
Τότε ἐμπρὸς εἰς τὸν λαόν, οἱ δύο γλῶσσα μία:
«Ἀκούσατε πᾶς ὁ λαὸς, ὅλοι οἱ Ἰουδαῖοι,
Καὶ ὅσοι ἤλθετε ἐδὼ, καὶ ξένοι καὶ Ἑβραῖοι.
Ὄντες ἡμεῖς οἱ δύο μας μέσα στὸ περιβόλι,
Περιπατοῦντες μοναχοὶ, μὲ τὸ νὰ λείπαν ὅλοι,
Ἦλθεν αὐτὴ μὲ δύο της δουλεύτραις καὶ ἐμπαίνει
Μέσα στὸ περιβόλιον, ὡς ἦτον μαθημένη.
Ἐμπαίνωντας δὲ, παρευθὺς, ἐκείναις ταῖς γυρίζει,
Ταῖς στέλνει πίσω καὶ ταῖς δυὸ, καμμίαν δὲν κρατίζει.
Καὶ κλείει τοῦ περιβολιοῦ εὐθὺς αὐτὴ ταῖς θύραις,
Ἀτή της μὲ ταῖς ἴδιαις ταῖς ἐδικαῖς της χεῖρες.
Καὶ ἀπὸ μέσα, παρευθὺς, εὐγαίνει ἕνας νέος,

24

Would have no room to fall, no room indeed.
People came and waited; they were all ears
To hear the verdict given by those brutes.
. . . .
Then the elders turned and spoke in unison,
In anger too and with a ringing voice:
"Send for Susanna, daughter of Hilkiah,
The wife of Joakim, our worthy master."
They sent for her at once and so she came,
Together with her children and her parents,
As well as all her relatives and servants,
Who clustered round and stayed next to her.
Susanna was supremely beautiful,
Exceptionally fair and young and tender.
To feast their eyes on her, the scoundrels who
Were godless men, thus ordered to unveil her.
. . . .

False testimony against Susanna
. . . .

And so, with hands positioned on her head,
The villains opened their befouled mouth
And spoke, loud and clear for all to hear,
Before the crowd; two men with voice united:
"O people, listen, all of you, all Jews
And those here present, foreigners and Hebrews.
While the two of us were in the garden,
Walking on our own, with no one else around,
This woman came with two handmaidens,
Entering the grove as was her custom.
But then she sent the maids back home at once,
Dismissed them both, not keeping even one.
She shut the garden gates immediately,
And did this by herself with her own hands.
Just then, a young man appeared from within

Καὶ τρέχει, πάγει θαρρετὰ, στοῦ λόγου της εὐθέως.
Τὴν πιάνει ἀπὸ τὸ χέρι της, εὐθὺς τὴν ἀγκαλιάζει,
Καὶ πέφτει μὲ τοῦ λόγου της ἀντάμα, καὶ πλαγιάζει.
Ἡμεῖς δὲ ὄντες καὶ οἱ δυὸ ἐκεῖ εἰς τὴν γωνίαν,
Ἰδόντες τὰ γινόμενα, αὐτὴν τὴν ἀνομίαν,
Ἐδράμαμεν ἀπάνω τους, μὲ περισσήν μας βίαν,
Καὶ εἴδαμεν ποῦ ἔκαμαν πλέον τὴν ἁμαρτίαν.
Ἐκεῖνον δὲν μπορέσαμεν, ἀλήθειαν λαλοῦμεν,
Νὰ τὸν κρατήσωμεν καλὰ καὶ νὰ τὸν ἐβαστοῦμεν,
Μὲ τὸ νὰ ἦτον δυνατὸς ἀπὸ ἡμᾶς, καὶ νέος,
Κἰ ἀνοίγωντας ἐπήδησε, καὶ ἔφυγε δρομαίως.
Ὅμως, πιάνωντες αὐτήν, ἡμεῖς, τὴν ἐκρατοῦμεν,
Καὶ νὰ μᾶς πῇ τί ἄνθρωπος ἦτον, τὴν ἐρωτοῦμεν.
Καὶ δὲν ἠθέλησε ποσῶς νὰ μᾶς τὸν φανερώσῃ,
Τὸ ὄνομά του νὰ μᾶς πῇ, μήπως καὶ τὸν προδώσῃ.
Ἐτοῦτα ὀφθαλμοφανῶς τὰ εἴχαμεν ἰδοῦμεν,
Ἐτοῦτα καὶ σᾶς λέγομεν ἡμεῖς, καὶ μαρτυροῦμεν.»
Ταῦτα ἐκεῖνοι λέγοντες ἔμπρὸς τῶν Ἰουδαίων,
Ἐπείσθη ἡ συναγωγὴ ἄπασα τῶν Ἑβραίων.
Ἐπίστευσαν οἱ ἄρχοντες αὐτοὺς ὡς πρεσβυτέρους,
Καὶ ὡς κριτὰς μὲν τοῦ λαοῦ, καὶ πλέον πιστωτέρους.
Διὸ κατέκριναν αὐτήν, εὐθὺς νὰ τελευτήσῃ,
Ὅλοι τους ἀπεφάσισαν, πῶς πλέον νὰ μὴ ζήσῃ.
«Ἀξία διὰ θάνατον,» εἶπαν, «θανατωθήτω!»
Κατὰ τὸν νόμον λέγοντες τὸ λιθοβοληθήτω.
Ἐβόησε δὲ μὲ φωνὴν μεγάλην ἡ Σωσάννα,
Καὶ εἶπε πρὸς τὸν Κύριον, μὲ γλῶσσα σὰν καμπάνα:
«Ὁ Θεὸς ὁ αἰώνιος, ὁ τῶν κρυφίων γνώστης,
Ἐσὺ Θεὲ καὶ Κύριε, ὁποῦ 'σαι ὁ προγνώστης,
Ὁποῦ τὰ πάντα ἀληθῶς ἠξεύρεις πρὶν γενοῦσι,
Καὶ τὰ γνωρίζεις ὡς καθὼς ὕστερ' ἀκολουθοῦσι,
Ἐσὺ γνωρίζεις, Κύριε, πῶς μὲ συκοφαντοῦσι,
Ψεύματα τοῦτοι σήμερον μὲ καταμαρτυροῦσι.
Καὶ νά, ὁποῦ πεθαίνω πλιό, εἶναι νὰ τελευτήσω,

And ran with bold steps directly to her.
He took her by the hand, embraced her
Straightaway, bent down and lay with her.
Now we were in the corner, both of us,
And when we saw this vileness taking place,
We ran toward them using all our might,
And witnessed them committing the greatest sin.
We could not seize the man—we speak in truth—
We could not get a hold of him at all,
For he was young and much too strong for us.
He opened the gate, jumped out and ran away.
We caught the woman though, took hold of her,
And asked her to inform us who he was.
She refused to make this known to us,
And did not say his name, lest she betray him.
These deeds we witnessed unmistakably,
These deeds we make known to you and testify."
While they were speaking thus before the Jews,
The entire congregation was persuaded.
The governors believed them as they were
The elders and trusted judges of the people.
And so at once they sentenced her to death,
All deciding that she should live no more.
"She must be put to death!" they said and meant,
According to the law, that she be stoned.
Susanna gave a loud and piercing cry,
And said to the Lord, with a tongue like a bell:
"Eternal God, you know what is secret;
My Lord and God, you know of things to come,
You know all things before they happen,
And know the things that happen afterward.
My Lord, you know that they discredit me;
These men today have lied against me.
And now I am to die, to breathe my last,

Δίχως νὰ κάμω τίποτες, καὶ δίχως νὰ ποιήσω.
Ἀπ᾽ ὅσα τοῦτοι κατ᾽ ἐμοῦ, εἶπαν μὲ πονηρίαν,
Λέγοντες πῶς μὲ εἴδασι, κ᾽ ἔκαμνα ἁμαρτίαν—»
Ταῦτα ἐπρόφθασε νὰ πῇ, κ᾽ εὐθὺς τὴν κατεβάζουν
Μέσα ἀπὸ τὸ σπῆτι της, καὶ ἔξω τὴν εὐγάζουν.
Καὶ τὴν πηγαίνουν, ἀδελφὲ, νὰ τὴν λιθοβολήσουν,
Καὶ τὴν πηγαίνουν, φίλε μου, γιὰ νὰ τὴν ἀφανίσουν.
Δὲν βγάζουν λείψανα ποτὲ, μὲ τόσον πολὺν θρῆνον,
Μὲ ὅσον εὔγαλαν αὐτὴν εἰς τὸν καιρὸν ἐκεῖνον.
Ὁ κόσμος ὅλος ἔκλαιε, καὶ κλαίωντας πηγαίνει,
Ἀκολουθεῖ κατώπιν της, καὶ ποῖος ἀπομένει;
Ἔκλειον τ᾽ ἀργαστήρια, ἄφιναν ταῖς δουλιαῖς τους
Οἱ ἄνθρωποι, καὶ πήγαιναν κατώπιν μὲ φωναῖς τους.
. . . .
«Θέε μου,» εἶπα ἐκ ψυχῆς, «Θεέ μου, καὶ δὲν κάνεις,
Διὰ τὸ δίκαιον αὐτῆς, τῆς ταπεινῆς Σωσάννης;»
. . . .
Ἀκόμι δὲν ἀπόσωσα τὸν λόγον, καὶ κοιτάζω
Πρᾶγμα ὁποῦ μὲ ἔφριξεν ὁ νοῦς νὰ τὸ λογιάζω.
Κοιτάζω, βλέπω, θεωρῶ, ἕνα παιδὶ εὐγαίνει
Μέσα στὴν μέσην τοῦ λαοῦ, καὶ κράζει, συντυχαίνει.
Ἕνα παιδὶ κράζει, βοᾷ—μὰ τίς νὰ τὸ γρικήσῃ;
Ἀπὸ τὴν τόσην σύγχυσιν, τί λέγει, νὰ νοήσῃ;
Καὶ τὸ παιδὶ, μικρὸ παιδὶ, δὲν ἤτονε μεγάλο,
Νὰ φαίνεται τὸ σῶμα του, ὡσὰν καὶ κάθε ἄλλο.
Καὶ ὅσοι δὲν τὸ ἔβλεπαν: «Ἀπὸ τὴν γῆν εὐγαίνει;
Ἤ οὐρανόθεν ἡ φωνή,» ἔλεγαν, «καταβαίνει;»
Ὁ κόσμος, ὁποῦ πρότερον εἶχε τὰ μάτια του
Καὶ τὴν Σωσάννα ἔβλεπε, κ᾽ ἐκεῖ ᾽τον ἡ καρδιά του,
Πλεὰ τότε τὴν ἀφήκασι, κὶ ἄρχησαν νὰ γυρεύουν
Τὸ στόμα κεῖνο τῆς φωνῆς, καὶ νὰ περισκοπεύουν.
Ἔπαυσαν καὶ τὰ κλάματα διὰ ν᾽ ἀκροασθοῦσι
Τὰ λόγια κεῖνα τῆς φωνῆς, τί εἶναι, τί ζητοῦσι.
«Ἄθῶος,» ἔλεγεν, «ἐγὼ ἀπὸ τοῦ αἵματός της,

Though I have not done anything at all.
Of all the things they slyly charge me with,
They claim they witnessed me committing sin—"
This much she managed to express before
They took her from her house and dragged her out.
My fellow brother, out they went to stone her,
Out they went to terminate her life.
No relic was displayed with such lament
As at that moment when they brought her out.
All were weeping, walking on in tears.
They went behind her—who was left behind?
The people shut their shops, they left their work
And went along with cries and lamentations.
· ·
And from my soul I said: "My God, my God
Will you not bring justice for poor Susanna?"
· ·
I hardly finished my words, when I saw
A sight that makes me shudder at the thought.
I look and see and I behold a child emerging
In the midst of all the people, shouting.
A child gave out a cry—but who could hear him?
In such commotion, who could understand him?
He was a small child, hardly big enough
To be conspicuous, as others were.
And those who could not see him said: "This voice—
Does it come from the earth or down from heaven?"
The crowd, which till that point had fixed their eyes
Upon Susanna, their hearts being there as well,
Now turned away and started searching for
The mouth that gave that voice; they looked around
And stopped their crying too, so they could listen
To that voice. What was it? What was it seeking?
"I am innocent of her blood," he said.

29

Ἄθῶος καὶ ἀμέτοχος εἶμαι ἐγὼ ἐμπρός της.»
Τοῦτο ὁ κόσμος νὰ το ἰδῇ, τοῦτο νὰ τὸ γρικήσῃ,
Γύρισαν ὅλοι στὸ παιδὶ, καὶ εἶχαν σταματήσῃ.
Καὶ λέγουσιν εἰς τὸ παιδὶ: «Τί λόγον συντυχαίνεις;
Πῶς τὸ ἐσύντυχες αὐτό; Μ᾽ αὐτὸ τί παρασταίνεις;»
Τὸ δὲ παιδὶ ἐστάθηκεν ἀνάμεσα στὸ πλῆθος
Μὲ ἕνα ἡγεμονικὸν, χαριτωμένον ἦθος.
Θαρρεῖς πῶς ἀγγελόπουλον ἦτον, κατεβασμένον
Μέσα ἀπὸ τοὺς οὐρανοὺς, εἰς τοῦτο ὡρισμένον.
Βέβαια ἐκινήθηκεν ὑπὸ τοῦ παναγίου,
Προσκυνητοῦ μου Πνεύματος, ὦ χάρις τοῦ παιδίου!
Καθὼς τὸ Πνεῦμα τὸ αὐτὸ, εἶχε ποτὲ κινήσῃ
Καὶ τὸ παιδὶ τὸν Σαμουὴλ, καὶ εἶχε τὸ ξυπνήσῃ,
Νὰ πῇ τὸν γέροντα Ἠλεὶ, ὅτι νὰ διορθώσῃ
Τὰ τέκνα του τὰ ἀπειθῆ, μήπως τὸν θανατώσῃ.
. . . .
Ὁ κόσμος ὁποῦ πήγαινε μὲ πόδια κομμένα,
Μὲ στόματα ὅλο φωναῖς, μὲ μάτια κλαμένα,
Ἔπαυσαν, ἐσιώπησαν, δὲν κλαῖν, δὲν ὀλολύζουν,
Τὰ πόδια τους δυνάμωσαν, τὰ μάτια τους σφο).γγίζουν.
Σπρώχνονται καὶ στριμώνονται, καθένας γιὰ νὰ φτάξῃ,
Νὰ ἰδῇ, ν᾽ ἀκούσῃ τὸ παιδὶ τί ἔχει νὰ προστάξῃ.

Κρίσις τοῦ Δανιὴλ
Τὸ δὲ παιδίον: «Ὦ ἐσεῖς, ἄρχοντες καὶ πρεσβύται
Καὶ ἅπας,» εἶπεν, «ὁ λαὸς, ὅλοι Ἰσραηλῖται,
Τόσον πολλὰ ἀνόητοι εἶσθε καὶ μωραμένοι,
Δίχως νὰ ἐξετάξετε καλὰ, καθὼς τυχαίνει,
Δίχως νὰ ἐρωτήσετε καταλεπτῶς, τελείως,
Καὶ νὰ γνωρίσετε σωστὰ τὸ πρᾶγμα, καὶ κυρίως,
Ἐκατακρίνατε ἐσεῖς γυναῖκα τιμημένην,
Καὶ θυγατέρα Ἰσραὴλ, καὶ θεοφοβουμένην.
Σταθῆτε, σταματήσετε, ἔχω νὰ σᾶς λαλήσω!
Κανεὶς μὴ πάγῃ ἀπὸ σᾶς, μπροστὰ, μὴ δὲ ὀπίσω.

"I am innocent and take no part before her."
The people wished to see and hear the child
So everybody turned to him and stopped.
And to the child they said: "What words are these?
How can you say this? Who do you claim to be?"
The child stood up in the midst of the crowd
In a dignified and graceful manner.
You would have thought he was a little angel,
Sent down from heaven for this purpose.
No doubt he had been moved by the power
Of the Holy Spirit—O grace of the child!—
As the Spirit itself had also once moved
The child called Samuel, awakening him
To tell the priest Eli that he should chasten
His unruly sons lest he be put to death.
. . . .
The crowd that moved before with heavy limbs,
With vociferous cries and tear-filled eyes,
Now stopped, was mute; they did not cry or wail.
Their limbs gained strength; they wiped their eyes.
They pushed and shoved each other as they tried
To see and hear what the child had to say.

The judgment of Daniel
The child thus spoke: "O leaders and elders,
And all people here, all Israelites!
How very foolish and unwise you are,
Without examining exhaustively,
Without investigating thoroughly
Or learning all the facts correctly,
That you should sentence a respected woman,
A God-fearing daughter of Israel.
Hold back and stop! I have to speak to you!
Let no one take a step forward or back.

Διότι τοῦτοι ἔκαμαν ψεύτικην μαρτυρίαν,
Ψευδῶς κατεμαρτύρισαν, καὶ διὰ πονηρίαν.»
....
Στέκουσιν ὅλοι μὲ σπουδὴν καὶ μ' ἀνοικτὰ ἀφτία
Ν' ἀκούσουν ὅλοι τοῦ παιδιοῦ τὰ λόγια του τὰ θεῖα.
Στέκεται δὲ καὶ τὸ παιδὶ αὐτό, συντροφιασμένον,
Μετὰ τῶν πρεσβυτέρων τε, καὶ πλέα τιμημένων.
Ἐστάθηκαν οἱ ἄρχοντες ἐκεῖ καὶ προσκαλοῦσι
Τὸν νέον τοῦτον τὸν κριτὴν, καὶ φρίττουν, ἀποροῦσι
Καὶ λέγουν: «Ὅρισαι ἐδὼ, στάσου ἀνάμεσά μας,
Καὶ λέγε καὶ ἀνάγγειλε τὸν λόγον ἐμπροστά μας.
Ὅτι ἐσένα ὁ Θεὸς, ἐσένα τὸ παιδίον,
Τὴν κρίσιν ταύτην ἔδωκε, καὶ ὅλον τὸ πρεσβεῖον.»
Τότε λοιπὸν ὁ Δανιὴλ λέγει: «Χωρίσατέ τους,
Μακρὰν ἕναν ἀπ' τὸν ἄλλον, εὐθὺς μακρύνατέ τους.
Καὶ νὰ τοὺς κρίνω αὐτουνούς, ἐγὼ νὰ τοὺς μιλήσω,
Ἕναν πρὸς ἕναν χωριστὰ, νὰ τοὺς ξομολογήσω.»
Ἀφ' οὗ ἐξεχωρίσθηκαν, ἕνας ἀπὸ τὸν ἄλλον,
Δαίμονας ἀπ' τὸν σατανᾶ, μὲ φόβον τους μεγάλον,
Κράζει τὸν ἕναν ἀπ' αὐτοὺς, καὶ λέγει: «Ὠργισμένε,
Γεμάτε ἡμερῶν κακῶν, καὶ πεπαλαιωμένε.
Τώρα σὲ ἔφθασαν, πικρὲ, ὅλαις ἡ ἁμαρτίαις
Ὁπό 'καμνες προτήτερα, κ' ἡ τόσαις ἀδικίαις
Κρίνωντας κρίσες ἄδικαις, ἀθώους κατακρίνων,
Τοὺς πταίστας ἀπολύωντας καὶ τοὺς κακοὺς ἀφίνων.
Καὶ ὅμως λέγει ὁ Θεὸς, καὶ σὺ τὸ διαβάζεις,
Ἀθῶον καὶ τὸν δίκαιον, νὰ μὴ καταδικάζῃς.
Τώρα, λοιπὸν, ἐὰν αὐτὴν τὴν εἶδες καθὼς λέγεις,
Καὶ ἔκαμνε τὸ πονηρὸν, ἀκάθαρτε, τί κλαίγεις;
Εἰπὲ, εἰς τί δένδρον, ἐσὺ, νὰ κάμνουν ἁμαρτίαν,
Τοὺς εἶδες μὲ τὰ μάτια σου; Εἰπὲ, μὲ ἀφοβίαν.»
Ἐκεῖνος ἀπεκρίθηκε: «Κάτω ἀπ' ἕνα σχοῖνον.»
Τὸν εἶπε δὲ ὁ Δανιὴλ, τὸν μιαρὸν ἐκεῖνον:
«Ἀλήθεια ψευμάτισες κατὰ τῆς κεφαλῆς σου,

For these men here gave false testimony.
Out of wickedness they gave false evidence."
....
All stood in earnest and with open ears
To listen to the child's celestial words.
The child itself stood too, surrounded by
The elders and the most distinguished men.
The leaders stood there and they summoned
This young judge; they shuddered, were astonished,
And they said: "Do come and stand among us,
And announce your message here before us.
Because to you, a mere child, has God
Bestowed this judgment and this privilege."
So Daniel then began: "Divide them both
And keep them far apart from one another.
I will speak to them, I will examine them,
Each one alone, and get them to confess."
When they were separated from each other,
Demons of the devil filled with terror,
He summoned one of them and said:
"You fiend, old relic full of wickedness,
Your sins have now caught up with you,
Misdeeds that you committed in the past:
Passing unjust verdicts, sentencing the blameless,
Acquitting the guilty and setting free the wicked.
But God has said, and you know it well:
'Do not condemn the just and innocent.'
Now if you really saw her, as you claim,
Committing sin, why do you weep, you filth?
Tell me, what tree was it where you caught sight
Of them committing sin? Speak, without fear!"
"It was a mastic tree," the man replied.
Then Daniel said to that befouled man:
"Indeed, you have just lied against your self,

Κακή, ἀθλία κεφαλή, καὶ κατὰ τῆς ψυχῆς σου.
Ὅτι ὁ ἄγγελος Θεοῦ στέκεται ἀοράτως,
Παίρνωντας ἀπὸ τὸν Θεὸν τὴν προσταγὴν τὸ κράτος.
Καὶ τώρα θέλει, βέβαια, στὴν μέσην νὰ σὲ σχίσῃ,
Τούτην τὴν ὥραν, φοβερά, νὰ σὲ διχοτομήσῃ.»
Εἶτα μετατοπίζωντας αὐτόν, εὐθὺς προστάσσει
Τὸν ἄλλον νὰ τὸν φέρουσι, διὰ νὰ τὸν ξετάσῃ.
Ὡσὰν τὸν ἔφεραν κί αὐτόν, πάλιν προοιμιάζει,
Αὐτὸς ἐκεῖνος ὁ κριτής, καὶ τὸν ἐγκωμιάζει.
Καὶ λέγει: «Σπέρμα Χαναάν, τοῦ κεκατηραμένου,
Καὶ ὄχι τοῦ Ἰούδα δὲ, τοῦ πανευλογημένου,
Τὸ κάλλος σὲ ἀπάτησε, μωρέ, κ' ἡ εὐμορφία,
Καὶ σὲ διέστρεψε τὸν νοῦν κακὴ ἐπιθυμία.
Ἔτζι ἐσεῖς ἐκάμνετε ταῖς ἄλλαις ταῖς Ὁβραΐσσας,
Κ' ἐκείναις, πάλιν, ἡ πτωχαῖς, τρελλαῖς, φοβούμεναίς σας,
Ἔκαμναν μὲ τοῦ λόγου σας, σκύλοι, τὴν ἁμαρτίαν,
Ἐτούτην τὴν ἀσέβειαν, καὶ τὴν παρανομίαν.
Αὐτὴ ὅμως δὲν ἔστερξε, δὲν εἶχεν ὑπομείνῃ
Αὐτὴ ἡ ἀνομία σας στοῦ λόγου της νὰ γίνῃ.
Λέγε με τώρα καὶ ἐσύ, γιατὶ καλὰ θυμᾶσαι,
Εἰς τί δένδρον τοὺς εὕρηκες; Βδέλυγμα, τί φοβᾶσαι;»
Ἐτοῦτος ἀπεκρίθηκε: «Κάτω ἀπ' ἕνα πρῖνον.»
Τὸν εἶπε δὲ ὁ Δανιήλ: «Ὁ ἄλλος εἶπε σχοῖνον.
Ψεῦσται, θεοκατάρατοι! Κατὰ τῆς κεφαλῆς σου
Ὀρθῶς καὶ σὺ ψευμάτησες, καὶ κατὰ τῆς ψυχῆς σου.
Ἰδοὺ στέκει ὁ ἄγγελος, καὶ σὲ νὰ πριονίσῃ,
Καὶ ἔτζι καὶ τοὺς δύο σας, μαζὶ νὰ ἀφανίσῃ.»
. . . .
Λιθοβολοῦνται οἱ κακόγεροι
Ταῦτα ἀκούσαντες εὐθύς, ὅλοι τους ὁμοφώνως
Ἐβόησαν, ἐφώναξαν, ἐκεῖ μεγαλοφώνως.
Καὶ τὸν Θεόν, τὸν σώζοντα ὅσους σ' αὐτὸν ἐλπίζουν,
Εὐλόγησαν, ἐδόξασαν, καὶ τὸν κριτὴν φημίζουν.
Καὶ ἐσυκώθηκαν εὐθὺς καὶ ἄρπαξαν δικαίως

A self depraved and vile; against your soul as well.
Because God's angel stands invisibly,
Receiving the decree and power from God.
His will is now that you be torn apart
This very hour, that you be cut in two."
Putting him aside, he ordered them at once
To bring the other man for questioning.
And when they brought him, he began again,
That very judge, to sing his praises.
He said: "You offspring of Canaan the cursed,
And not of Judah which is blessed on high!
O fool, beguiled by beauty and good looks,
How evil passion led your mind astray.
You did the same to other daughters of Israel,
And they, being senseless, poor, and scared
Of you, committed sin with you, you hounds!
They committed this profanity and crime.
But she did not consent; she did not allow
This wickedness of yours to come to pass.
Do tell me now, for you remember well,
The tree where you observed them. Why fear, vile thing?"
And he replied: "It was an oak tree."
Daniel said: "The other said a mastic tree.
Liars and accursed ones! Against your self
You too have lied, against your soul as well.
Behold the angel stands to saw you down,
And so destroy the two of you together."
. . . .
The evil elders are stoned
Hearing this at once, everyone together
Raised their voice and gave a roaring shout.
And to God, who saves whoever hopes in him,
They gave thanks and glory, and praised the judge.
They rose at once and justly seized with force

Ἐκείνους τοὺς κακόγερους, ἀλύπητα, βιαίως.
Διότι τοὺς ὑπόστησεν ὁ Δανιὴλ ὁ θεῖος,
Ὡς εἶπον, ψευδομάρτυρας ἐκ στόματος κυρίως.

Καὶ ἐν ταυτῷ τοὺς πέρνουσι, τοὺς σέρνουν, τοὺς βιάζουν,
Καὶ ἐν ταυτῷ ὅλοι ὁμοῦ φωνάζουν, ἀλαλάζουν.

Καὶ γίνεται ἕνα κακὸν, καὶ γίνετ᾽ ἕνα τέρας,
Ὁποῦ θαρρῶ δὲν ἔγινε ποτὲ σ᾽ ἄλλας ἡμέρας.

Ὥρμησαν, καὶ ἐχύθηκαν τόσα πολλὰ κορμία,
Εἰς δυὸ κορμία μοναχὰ, κὶ αὐτὰ τόσον ἀχρεῖα.

Κ᾽ ἐκεῖ τοὺς ἐκτυπήσασιν ἕνα διαβολισμένο
Πετρίδι, τῆς ὀργῆς Θεοῦ, καὶ κατατρομασμένο.

Κακοὺς κακῶς ἀπώλεσαν, κατὰ τὸ γεγραμμένον,
Κατὰ τὰ ἔργατα αὐτῶν, τῶν ἐντροπιασμένων.

Γυναῖκες νὰ ταῖς ἔβλεπες, χώματα ξύλ᾽ ἁρποῦσαν,
Καὶ ἔρριχναν ἀπάνω τους, τοὺς ἀσχημολογοῦσαν.

Πολλαῖς, καϊμέναις ἀπ᾽ αὐτοὺς, καὶ πλιὸ δὲν τὸ βαστοῦσαν,
Εὔγαζαν τὰ παπούτζια τους, κ᾽ ἔτρεχαν, τοὺς κτυποῦσαν.

Καὶ οὕτως ἔγινε σ᾽ αὐτοὺς ἡ ἰδία παιδεία,
Ὁποῦ αὐτοὶ ἑτοίμαζαν εἰς ἄλλον ἀδικία.

. . . .

Καθὼς λιθοβολίσθηκαν ἐτοῦτ᾽ οἱ δυὸ ἀξίως,
Καὶ ἔδωκαν εἰς τοὺς μοιχοὺς παράδειγμα κυρίως,
Τὸ αἷμα δὲ τὸ ἄπταιστον ἐγλύτωσεν, ἐσώθη,
Καὶ ἡ Σωσάννα ἔζησε, κ᾽ ἡ δόξα της ἁπλώθη.

Καὶ ἔδωκεν εἰς τὰς καλὰς γυναῖκας, καὶ τιμίας,
Δύναμιν καὶ παράδειγμα καὶ τύπον πολιτείας.

Χελκίας ὁ πατέρας της, ὁμοῦ δὲ καὶ ἡ μάνα,
Ἐδόξασαν τὸν Κύριον πολλὰ γιὰ τὴν Σωσάννα,
Καὶ ὁ καλός της ἄνδρας της μετὰ τῶν συγγενῶν του,
Καὶ ὅλων τῶν ἀνθρώπων του, καὶ τῶν οἰκειακῶν του.

Ὁ κόσμος τὴν ἐχαίρουνταν καὶ τὴν ἐχαιρετοῦσαν,
Κ᾽ ἕναν χορὸν, δὲν ἄργησαν, θωρῶ, κ᾽ ἐσυγκροτοῦσαν.
Ἡ μάνα κὶ ὁ πατέρας της τὴν ἐγλυκοφιλοῦσαν,
Οἱ συγγενεῖς, οἱ ἐδικοὶ, πολλὰ τὴν ἐτιμοῦσαν.

Those evil elders, feeling no remorse.
For Daniel the divine had proved that they
Committed perjury from their own mouths.
They were then seized and dragged and hustled,
As the people all together bawled and blared.
Then something dire and hideous occurred
That never had occurred, I think, before.
The multitude of people charged and pounced
Upon the two lone men, these loathsome men.
And there they flung at them a stone of fear
And outrage, moved by the wrath of God.
They slew them fiercely according to the law,
According to their deeds, disgraceful men.
The women were a sight! Grabbing soil and sticks,
They hurled these at them, cursing all along.
Many, who had suffered, could bear it no more;
They doffed their shoes and ran and pounded them.
And so these men received the very punishment
That they were wrongfully preparing for another.
. . . .
As these two men had rightfully been stoned,
Providing an example to adulterers,
Susanna's blameless blood was spared and saved,
And she survived, her glory spreading far.
To fair and virtuous women she gave strength,
A paragon and model of decorum.
Hilkiah her father, and her mother too,
Did greatly praise the Lord for their Susanna.
So did her kindly husband and his relatives,
As well as all his people and his household.
People rejoiced in her and greeted her
And they prepared a dance without delay.
Her mother and her father kissed her fondly,
Her relatives and close ones honored her.

Ὅλοι τὴν ἐμακάριζαν, ὅλοι τὴν ἐπαινοῦσαν,
Καὶ ὅλοι τὴν ἐθαύμαζαν, καὶ ὑπεραποροῦσαν.
Δοῦλοι, δουλεύτραις, γείτονες, ὅλοι τὴν προσκυνοῦσαν,
Καὶ ὡς ἁγίαν, πάντοτε, τὴν εἶχαν, τὴν θωροῦσαν.
Ἐγύρισεν ἡ λύπη τους εἰσὲ χαρὰν μεγάλην,
Ἡ ἐντροπὴ εἰς δόξαν τους, παρὰ καμμίαν ἄλλην.
....
Τὰ δὲ παιδάκια της μικρὰ, κὶ εὔμορφα σὰν τὴν μάνα,
Αὐτὰ πρῶτα ἀγκάλλιασε μὲ πόθον ἡ Σωσάννα.
Κ' ἐκεῖ ὁποῦ τὰ χαίρουνταν καὶ τὰ γλυκοφιλοῦσε,
Καὶ μὲ τὸν ἄνδρα της γλυκὰ, δὲν ξεύρω τί μιλοῦσε,
Τρέχω πηγαίνω καὶ ἐγὼ, καὶ τῆς φιλῶ τὸ χέρι,
Καὶ πάραυτα μ' ἐγνώρισε, γιατὶ μὲ εἶχε ξεύρη.
Τὴν ἐσυγχάρηκα κ' ἐγὼ, μ' ὅλην μου τὴν καρδίαν,
Καὶ λέγω της μὲ πᾶσαν μου χαρὰν καὶ θυμηδίαν:
«Εὐλογητὸς ὁ Κύριος, ὁποῦ τὴν προσευχήν σου
Ἐδέχθηκε καὶ ἔσωσε τὴν καθαρὰν ζωήν σου.
Καὶ ἐσυγχώρησεν αὐτὸς ἐκεῖνα νὰ γενῶσιν,
Ἐσὺ διὰ νὰ τιμηθῇς, κ' ἐκεῖνοι νὰ χαθῶσιν.
Ἐκεῖνοι καθὼς ἄξιοι ἀπὸ πολλῆς θανάτου,
Σὺ ὡς ἀξία δὲ τιμῆς καὶ μνήμης ἀθανάτου.»

She was blessed by all and praised by all,
And all admired her, feeling mystified.
Slaves, maids, and neighbours all adored her
Regarding her at all times as a saint.
Their sadness turned to overwhelming joy,
Their shame to glory, as never before.
. . . .
Her little children, handsome like their mother,
With fervent love Susanna first embraced.
And as she was rejoicing and caressing them,
And talking sweetly with her husband,
I made my way to her and kissed her hand.
She recognized me since she knew of me.
I congratulated her with all my heart
And told her with great joy and merriment:
"Blessed is the Lord, who heard your prayer,
Accepted it and saved your spotless life.
And he allowed those things to happen thus,
That you may be revered and they destroyed.
While they are most deserving of their death,
You merit praise and undying remembrance."

ΚΗΠΟΣ ΧΑΡΙΤΩΝ/
GARDEN OF GRACES

ΚΕΦΑΛΑΙΟΝ ΠΕΜΠΤΟΝ*
Περὶ τῆς ἐκ τοῦ κόσμου φυγῆς καὶ τῶν μετ᾽ αὐτὴν

Εἰς τοὺς πενῆντα δὲ καὶ τρεῖς ἐλθὼν στὸν ἑαυτόν μου,
στάθηκα κι ἐστοχάσθηκα τὰ πλήθη τῶν κακῶν μου
τῆς Μπογδανιᾶς καὶ τῆς Βλαχιᾶς, μάλιστα Μπογδανίας,
τέλος δὲ καὶ τῆς Πόλεως, πλήθη ἐπ᾽ ἀληθείας
ὁποὺ ὁ Δούναβις αὐτὸς νὰ τὰ ξεπλύνη ὅλος,
νὰ μὲ πιστέψῃς, δὲν ἀρκεῖ, ὄχι, ἀναμφιβόλως·
καὶ τὸ τοῦ κόσμου μάταιον ἰδὼν καὶ λογαριάσας,
καὶ τὰ τοῦ κόσμου πράγματα καλὰ κακὰ χορτάσας,
καὶ κόσμον καὶ ἐγκόσμια μὲ δίκαιο μισήσας,
ἀπὸ τὸν κόσμον ἔφυγα, ἔρημον ἀγαπήσας.
Ἀπὸ τὴν Πόλιν κίνησα, καὶ ἦλθα στὸ Πιπέρι
Αὐγούστου δέκα, νύχτα δὲ καὶ ὄχι μεσημέρι.
Εἶναι νησὶ παντέρημο μὲ δύο ἐκκλησίας,
τὴν νέαν καὶ τὴν παλαιάν, κ᾽ οἱ δυὸ τῆς Παναγίας·
καθὼς κ᾽ εἰς ἄλλα ὅμοια νησιὰ ἐκεῖ πλησίον
εὑρίσκονται ναοὶ δυὸ τρεῖς μὲ ἔλεος τὸ θεῖον·
καὶ ἔχουσι τὴν Σκόπελον αὐτὰ κ᾽ εἶναι καμπόσα,
ὡς τὰ παιδιὰ τὴν μάννα τους, σὰν τὰ πουλιὰ τὴν κλῶσσα.
Εἰς ταὶς εἰκοσιέξι δὲ μηνὸς τοῦ Ὀκτωβρίου,
ἀνήμερα τὴν ἑορτὴν τ᾽ ἁγίου Δημητρίου,
ὡς ἔθος ἐκουρεύθηκα, κουρεύματα νὰ ἔχω,
τὴν χάριν τῆς μοναδικῆς τάχατες νὰ μετέχω.
. . . .
Ἔμεινα μῆνας ἔξ ἑπτὰ ἀντάμα μὲ τοὺς ἄλλους
ὡς δέκα ὄντας ἀδελφούς, μικρούς τε καὶ μεγάλους,
ἀπέκει μ᾽ ἐξεχώρισαν ὡσὰν τὸ ψωριασμένον

---

* The extracts that follow are based on the edition of Legrand 1881 and correspond to lines 1–22, 31–72, and 107–36 of Book Five. Those from Book Eleven correspond to lines 1–120, 223–72, and 285–98. I have made only minor alterations (capitalization, word separation, punctuation), and for the most part have retained the original spelling.

BOOK FIVE
On My Withdrawal from the World

In seventeen fifty-three I came to myself
And stopped to recollect the sum of all the sins
I had committed in Moldavia and Wallachia
And Constantinople too. So many were my sins,
The entire Danube, without a doubt,
Would not suffice to wash them all away.
Perceiving then how futile this world was,
Surfeited with the good and bad things of this world,
My worldly ways I duly came to loathe,
And left the world, desiring solitude.
Departing from the City, I arrived
On Piperi at night, on August tenth.
It is a desert isle with two churches
Of the Virgin, a new and an old one.
Just as on the other islands nearby
Two or three churches exist, by God's grace.
These many islets surround Skopelos
As children a mother, or chicks a hen.
On the twenty-sixth day of October,
On the feast day of Saint Demetrios,
I took the tonsure, as is the custom,
And received the gift of celibacy.
. . . .
I stayed for six to seven months among
The brethren, ten in all, both young and old.
After that they set me apart, poor me,

τὸ πρόβατον τὸ ἴδιο κ᾽ ἐμένα τὸν καϊμένον.
Ὁ προεστὼς τῶν ἀδελφῶν μ᾽ ἔστειλε στὸ κελλίον,
ὁποὺ ξαργοῦ τὸ ἔκαμε πάλιν ἐκεῖ πλησίον·
καὶ κάνω ὁλομόναχος κοντὰ δυό ᾽μισυ χρόνους,
πλὴν ὄχι μὲ τοὺς πρέποντας μονα[χ]ικῆς τοὺς πόνους,
ξηγῶντας καὶ συνθέτοντας λόγους καὶ ἱστορίας
καὶ ὕμνους καὶ ἐγκώμια, καὶ διὰ στιχουργίας,
ὡς εἰς τοὺς τόμους φαίνονται ὑπὲρ τοὺς δέκα ὄντας,
ὁποῦ, ἂν ἴσως ἀγαπᾷς, θέλεις τοὺς βρεῖ ζητῶντας.
Καὶ βλέποντας τοὺς ἀδελφοὺς μόνον στὴν ἐκκλησίαν,
τὴν Κυριακή, καὶ στὸ φαγί, κι εὐθὺς στὴν μοναξίαν,
ζῶντας κατὰ ἀλήθειαν μὲ ἄκραν ἡσυχίαν,
ἐκεῖνο ὁποὺ ἤθελα, καὶ μὲ ἀμεριμνίαν,
καὶ γράφοντας καὶ σκάφτοντας· ζωή, τῇ ἀληθείᾳ,
ὡς λέγουν, χαρισάμενη, καὶ μία βασιλεία.
Ὁπόταν ἐκουράζουμουν ἐγὼ πλέον νὰ γράφτω,
ἔπαιρνα τὸ τζαπάκι μου, ἀρχίνιζα νὰ σκάφτω,
καὶ ἦτον τὸ ἐργόχειρο καὶ τζάπα καὶ κοντύλι,
καὶ πῶς νὰ ᾽ποῦν τόσα καλὰ μόνον τὰ δυό μου χείλη;
καὶ πῶς νὰ σοῦ διηγηθοῦν μετὰ λεπτολογίας
τοῦ Πιπεριοῦ μου τὰ καλὰ αὐτῆς τῆς τριετίας;

Περὶ τοῦ βασιλέως τῆς Ῥώμης
Θυμούμουν, ὅταν ἔσκαφτα, πάντα τὸν βασιλέα,
τὸ ὄνομά του ξέχασα, ὑπόθεσις ἀρχαία,
ὁποὺ τὸν θρόνον ἄφηκεν, εἶχεν ἀναχωρήση
εἰς ἕνα τζιφτιλίκι του, ἐκεῖ πῆγε νὰ ζήσῃ·
καὶ οἱ τῆς Ῥώμης ἄρχοντες τοῦ πῆγαν τὸ στεφάνι,
παρακαλοῦν νὰ τὸ δεχθῇ καὶ πάλιν νὰ τὸ βάνη,
καὶ νὰ γυρίσῃ εἰς αὐτούς, νὰ βασιλεύσῃ πάλιν,
ὅτι ἡ Ῥώμη τὸν ζητεῖ μ᾽ ἀγάπην της μεγάλην·
τὸν ηὗραν εἰς τὸν κῆπον δὲ, καὶ ἀνασκουμπωμένος
ἐσκάλιζε τὰ λάχανα χαίροντας, ξεννοιασμένος.
«Ἀφῆτε με, εἶπεν αὐτός, βλέπετε δὲν ἀδειάζω,

As if I were a black sheep, rank and foul.
The head of the monks sent me to my cell
Doing the same on purpose over again.
In solitude for two years and a half,
But suffering not the true trials of a monk,
I penned a mass of fables, stories, hymns
And eulogies, indited all in verse.
These now appear in volumes more than ten,
Which you may find if you wish to seek.
I only saw my brothers during church,
On Sundays, during meals, and then withdrew.
In truth, I lived my days in total silence,
Doing the things that pleased me, free of care:
Both writing and digging—a blissful life
As they say, it was a kingdom indeed.
Whenever I grew weary writing verse
I would take my little spade and start to dig.
It was my handiwork, the spade and pen.
How can my lips alone convey the happiness,
How can they tell in all its fullness
The bliss I felt for three years on Piperi?

The king of Rome
While digging, I always thought of that king
Whose name I don't recall—an old story—
Who left behind his throne and had withdrawn
To one of his farms and went there to live.
And the lords of Rome brought to him the crown,
Beseeching him to wear it once again,
To return to Rome and there resume the throne:
The city loved him and did want him back.
They found him in the garden, sleeves rolled-up,
Weeding his greens, carefree and content.
"Leave me alone!" he said. "I'm idling not,

γιατὶ τὰ κρομμυδάκια μου σκαλίζω καὶ κυττάζω,
νὰ πιάσω τὸ στεφάνι σας διὰ νὰ τὸ φορέσω,
ἀφῆτε με νὰ ζῶ ἐδῶ ἐγὼ καθὼς μπορέσω.»
Καὶ ἔλεγα ἂν ἤρχουνταν κ᾽ ἐμὲ νὰ μὲ γυρέψουν,
Βλάχμπεη νὰ μὲ κάμουσι καὶ νὰ μὲ ἀφεντέψουν,
«ἀφῆτε με, ἤθελα 'πεῖ, τὰ σκόρδα νὰ φυτεύω,
καιρὸν δὲν ἔχω Βλάχμπεης νὰ γένω, ν᾽ ἀφεντεύω.»
. . . .

Ἐγκώμιον ἐρημίας καὶ μοναχικῆς διαγωγῆς
Καὶ ἕνα τζεκουρόπουλο εἶχα κ᾽ ἐκαθερνοῦσα
πεύκια, ἐληαὶς, πρινάρια, καὶ ὅλο πελεκοῦσα,
καὶ ποτ᾽ ἐληαὶς ἐφύτευα, ποτ᾽ ἀχλαδιαὶς δὲ πάλιν,
ποτὲ μηλιαὶς, ἀμυγδαλιαὶς, μὲ δόξαν μου μεγάλην,
ποτὲ δὲ καὶ λαχανικὰ, πρασάκια καὶ σκορδάκια,
κ᾽ ἐχαίρουμουν στὰ χώματα, καθὼς σὺ στὰ φλωράκια.
Μέσα εἰς ἕνα βρίσκουμουν ἐγὼ κῆπον χαρίτων,
σ᾽ ἕνα παράδεισον τρυφῆς, αὐτὸ ἀλήθεια ἦτον·
καὶ πότε ἐκατέβαινα κ᾽ ἔβγαζα πεταλίδαις,
κοχύλια, καβούρια, κάποτε καὶ καρίδαις·
καὶ εἰς αὐτὰ πλειὸ χαίρουμουν παρὰ στὰις ἀρχοντιαίς μου,
στ᾽ ἀφεντικὰ συμπόσια καὶ ταὶς ἀρχόντισσαίς μου.
Ὁ Ἀρταξέρξης μιὰ φορά, ὁ βασιλεὺς Περσίας,
σῦκα καὶ κρίθινο ψωμὶ ηὗρεν ἐπ᾽ ἐρημίας,
καὶ τρώγοντας μὲ ὄρεξιν, διότι ἐπεινοῦσε·
«ὦ νοστιμάδα φαγητοῦ, ἔλεγ᾽, ἐμαρτυροῦσε,
κ᾽ ἐγὼ δὲν τὴν ἐγνώριζα ὡς τώρα στὸν καιρόν μου».
Τὸ ἴδιο ἔλεγα κ᾽ ἐγὼ πολλάκις στὸν θεόν μου·
καὶ ἤμουν πρὸς τὸν Κύριον ὅλο εὐχαριστία,
καὶ εἶχε μίαν ἡδονὴν ἄρρητον ἡ καρδία,
ὁ τόπος νὰ μοσχοβολᾷ, τὰ δένδρα νὰ μυρίζουν,
καὶ τὰ πουλάκια καὶ αὐτὰ νὰ σὲ κλωθογυρίζουν
νὰ ψάλλῃς σὺ τὸ ψαλτικὸ, νὰ κελαδοῦν ἐκεῖνα,
καὶ μὲ διάφορα ἡ γῆ λουλούδια καὶ κρίνα,

But tending to my onions in delight.
I cannot take and wear the crown you bring;
So leave, and let me live here as I wish."
I thought that even if they came for me
And asked that I be hospodar, I'd say:
"Please leave, for I am planting garlic now;
I have no time to serve as hospodar."
. . . .

In praise of solitude and the monastic life
I had a little axe with which I pruned
And chopped down trees of olive, pine and oak.
At times I planted pear and olive trees
Or apple trees and almond trees
And sometimes garlic, vegetables and leeks,
Rejoicing in the soil as you in coins.
I found myself in a garden of graces
A paradise of pleasures, truly so.
At times I went down to the sea
To gather limpets, shells and crabs and shrimps
And revelled in these things far more than in
The women, wealth and feasts I had in court.
The King of Persia, Artaxerxes, once
Found barley bread and figs in the desert,
And ate with relish, hungry as he was.
"How exquisite a taste is this!" he said.
"Such food I never savoured until now."
I often said the same to my own God
For whom my heart was filled with gratitude
And with a joy that words cannot express.
The place was fragrant, the trees full of scent,
And the birds themselves flitted about you;
As you chanted the psalms, they chirped away.
The earth was covered in lilies and flowers.

47

ἐτοῦτα νὰ εὐφραίνουσι τὴν ὅρασιν, τὰ μάτια,
θυμοῦμαι τα καὶ καίομαι καὶ γίνομαι κομμάτια·
ἐκεῖνα δὲ τὴν ἀκοὴν καὶ νὰ ἀναγαλλιάζῃς,
καὶ δὶς τὴν ὥρα τὸν θεὸν νὰ πέφτῃς νὰ δοξάζῃς·
ἀκοὴ, ὅρασις, ἀφὴ καὶ ὅσφρησις νὰ χαίρῃ,
εὐχαριστίαν πρὸς θεὸν καὶ δόξαν ν' ἀναφέρῃ.

The latter delighted one's sight, one's eyes
(I recall these and am aflame with joy).
The others enraptured one's hearing.
Twice each hour you fell to your knees in praise
Rejoicing in hearing, sight, touch and smell
Giving to God thanks and adoration.

ΚΕΦΑΛΑΙΟΝ ΕΝΔΕΚΑΤΟΝ
Περιγραφὴ τῆς Σάμου ἐπαινετικὴ

Πολλὰς νήσους ἐγύρισα, χώρας καὶ πολιτείας
ἀνατολῆς καὶ δύσεως, Εὐρώπης καὶ Ἀσίας,
καὶ εἰς πολλὰς εἶδα πολλὰ καλὰ ὁμοῦ καὶ κάλλη·
δόξαν νὰ ἔχῃ ὁ θεός, ἡ δόξα του μεγάλη!
ὡσὰν τῆς Σάμου τὰ πολλὰ καλὰ καὶ εὐμορφίας,
ὡσὰν τῆς Σάμου τὰ βουνὰ καὶ τὰς τοποθεσίας
δὲν εἴδασι τὰ μάτια μου, δὲν εἴδασι ποτέ μου,
ὡς τόσον εἶναι θαυμαστὸ νησί, πιστεύσατέ μου,
παράδεισον ἂν τὴν εἰπῇς, ἀληθινὰ τῆς πρέπει,
καὶ γῆν ἐπαγγελίας δὲ ὁπῴχει μάτια βλέπει.
Καὶ τὴν φυτεύει ὁ θεὸς κοντὰ εἰς τὴν Ἀσίαν,
νὰ τὴν τιμήσῃ καὶ μ' αὐτὸ τὴν νῆσον τὴν τιμίαν.
Ἐδῶ θωρεῖς, ἀγαπητέ, πλουσίους ἐλαιῶνας,
ἐδῶ θωρεῖς, ἀκροατά, μοσχάτους ἀμπελῶνας,
ὁποῦ γεμίζει ἡ Φραγκιὰ καὶ ὅλ' ἡ Μοσχοβία
μοσχάτο τὸ σαμιώτικο, νέκταρ τῇ ἀληθείᾳ·
τὴν ὑπερβαίν' ἡ Σκόπελος στὸ μαῦρο δίχως ἄλλο,
ἡ Σάμος στὸ μοσχάτο δέ, ποσῶς δὲν ἀμφιβάλλω.
Ἐδῶ, χρυσέ μου μπεγζαδέ, θωρεῖς λόφους, κοιλάδαις,
νερὰ πολλά, λόγγους πολλούς, γῆν ὅλον πρασινάδαις·
ἐδῶ θωρεῖς, Ἀλέξανδρε, μετ' ἄκρας ἀπορίας,
ὄρη μὲ σπήλαια πολλά, σπήλαια μ' ἐκκλησίας·
ἐδῶ σου κάνει τὸ νησὶ μὲ τὴν γειτόνισσά του
Ἀνατολὴν ἕνα πολλὰ στενὸ ἀντίκρυτά του,
στενώτερο ἀπ' τὸ στενὸ τῆς Πόλης δίχως ἄλλο,
κοντότερο ὅμως πολλά, ὄχι μακρύ, μεγάλο·
τόσο στενὸ ὥστε ὁποὺ ἡ Σάμος κ' ἡ Ἀσία
ἐδένουνταν καὶ δένεται καὶ νῦν ἐν εὐκολίᾳ·
ὡσὰν νὰ 'πῇς δυὸ ἀδελφαὶς πολλὰ ἠγαπημέναις,
μὲ τὴν ἀγάπην τὴν πολλὴν σὰν μὲ σχοινὶ δεμέναις,
καθὼς ποτὲ ὁ Γαλατᾶς καὶ τὸ Βυζάντιόν μας

BOOK ELEVEN
In Praise of Samos

Many are the islands, cities and countries
I have been to, as far as Asia in the East
And Europe in the West, where many things
So fair I found—o glory be to God!—
But anything as fair as the isle of Samos,
As the mountain peaks and sites of Samos,
My eyes have never set upon before.
Believe me, the isle is unique,
One would be right to call it Paradise
Or, setting eyes on it, the Promised Land.
God placed it close to Asia's shores, so that
The island's honor may be magnified.
Dear listener, right here you can behold
Rich olive groves and vineyards smelling sweet
That fill the whole of Moscow and the West
With Samian muscat, like nectar indeed.
Skopelos surpasses Samos in red wine,
But Samian muscat is by far the best.
Young bey, you may behold here dales and hills
And many forests, streams and pastures green.
Here, Alexandros, you can feast your eyes
On churches set in many mountain caves.
Here, with its neighbouring Asian coast,
The island forms a very narrow strait,
A strait more narrow than the Bosphorus
By far, but shorter, neither long nor large;
So narrow that where Samos and Asia
Used to join, could easily do so now.
Two sisters they resemble, bound by love,
A love that seems to bind them with a rope,
Like Galata and our Byzantium,

εἰς τὸν χρυσὸν αἰῶνα μας, ἢ εἰς τὸ ὄνειρόν μας.
Κ' ἕνα νησὶ καταμεσῆς μικράκι μ' ἐκκλησίαν
τ' ἁγίου Νικολάου δέ, ἄκουσα λειτουργίαν·
ἐδῶ κοντὰ ἕνα καιρὸν σοῦ εἶχεν ἕνα κάστρο,
ὁποῦ στὸν κόσμο ἔλαμπε ποτὲ σὰν ἕνα ἄστρο,
ἑλληνικό, παμπάλαιο, πολὺ τῇ ἀληθείᾳ
διὰ τὸ μεγαλεῖον του, καὶ πύργους καὶ τοιχεῖα,
μὲ πέτραις μεγαλώταταις αὐτὰ ὅλα κτισμένα,
ἀνδρείας τῆς ἑλληνικῆς καθρέφτης τὸ καθένα.
Τἄβλεπα καὶ ἐθαύμαζα, κ' ἐλεεινολογοῦσα
τὸ γένος μας τὸ τωρινό, καὶ ἐδακρυρροοῦσα·
καὶ ὄντως ἀνθρωπάρια, πίθηκας, μασκαράδαις
ὠνόμαζα τοῦ λόγου μας, κνώδαλα καὶ μαυράδαις.
Θέλ' εἶναι βεβαιότατα ὡς τρεῖς χιλιάδες χρόνοι
καὶ στέκεται τὸ κτίριο, καὶ φαίνεται δὲν λυόνει·
καὶ τὰ δικά μας δὲν περνᾷ χρόνος καὶ ἀρχινίζουν
νὰ σπάζουν, νὰ ραγίζωνται, καὶ νὰ κοντοκρημνίζουν·
κ' ἔχομεν μίαν ἔπαρσιν ἡμεῖς μὲν οἱ σπουδαῖοι,
πώς καὶ αὐτὸν τὸν Πλάτωνα περνοῦμεν οἱ χυδαῖοι·
οἱ ῥήτορες Κικέρωνα ὁμοῦ καὶ Ἰσοκράτην,
οἱ ἰατροί μας Γαληνόν ἴσως καὶ Ἱπποκράτην,
οἱ φρόνιμοί μας Νέστορα ἢ καὶ τὸν Παλαμήδη,
αὐτοὶ δὲ οἱ κτιστάδες μας αὐτὸν τὸν Ἀρχιμήδη.
Θεέ μου παντοδύναμε, ἢ γνῶσιν νὰ μᾶς δώσῃς,
ἢ κἂν νὰ στείλῃς ἀπ' τὴν γῆν ὅλους νὰ μᾶς σηκώσῃς·
γιατὶ καὶ τὴν ἁγίαν γῆν νὰ τὴν καταπατοῦμεν,
ἀνάξιοι γῆς εἴμεσθεν, ἀνάξιοι νὰ ζοῦμεν
   Ἐδῶ καὶ μίαν, τέκνον μου, κολώνα σου σηκώνει,
ὁποὺ, θαρρεῖς, στὰ σύγνεφα μέσα ἐκεῖ τὴν χώνει,
καὶ ὑψηλὴν καὶ θαυμαστὴν διὰ τὰ μεγαλεῖα,
τῶν λίθων ὄντων δώδεκα, τέρας τῇ ἀληθείᾳ·
τεράστιον ἀληθινὰ εἶναι αὐτὴ ἡ στήλη,
σωστὰ νὰ τὴν διηγηθῇ δὲν δύναται κοντύλι·
ἀπ' τὰ ἑπτὰ θεάματα τῆς γῆς νὰ εἶναι ἕνα

In our golden age or in our dream.
In the middle is an islet with a church
Of St. Nicholas; I heard a service there.
Nearby there once used to be a temple
Shining like a star throughout the world.
Greek it was, from ancient times indeed;
A striking one whose walls and columns were
Constructed with colossal slabs of stone;
A reflection of the ancient Greeks' prowess.
I looked at these admiringly and grieved,
Lamenting at our people's present state.
A pitiable lot I say we are: apes
And shammers, wretches and good-for-nothings.
About three thousand years have passed since then
The building, though, still stands: it is there, erect,
Whereas time hardly passes by
And ours begin to crumble, crack, collapse.
We have the arrogance to think that we
Surpass in greatness Plato; that orators
Surpass Isocrates and Cicero,
Our doctors Galen and Hippocrates,
Our wise men Nestor and Palamedes,
And our architects old Archimedes.
O God almighty, either give us sense
Or from the earth remove us altogether,
For we no longer merit or deserve
To dwell or tread upon this sacred earth.
    Right here, my son, one pillar soars so high
It seems to penetrate the clouds above,
Imposing in its height, a wondrous sight;
A dozen drums it has—monstrous indeed.
Truly towering, the pillar's height
In writing here can hardly be described.
This pillar should have been included in

ἡ στήλη ἔπρεπεν αὐτή, ὄντως βεβαιωμένα,
ἤ κἂν ὄγδοον θέαμα νὰ τὴν ὀνοματίσουν
τὴν στήλην τὴν σαμιώτικην, καὶ νὰ τὴν ἐψηφίσουν.
Ἀπὸ μακρόθεν ὥραις δυὸ τὴν βλέπεις καὶ σὲ κράζει
νὰ πᾷς διὰ νὰ τὴν ἰδῇς θαρρεῖς καὶ σὲ φωνάζει·
ὁ κάθε ἕνας λίθος της (ἄκουε καὶ νὰ φρίττῃς,
καὶ νὰ χαρῇς τὰ μάτια σου, παντοῦ νὰ τὴν κηρύττῃς)
ὀκτὼ ἐννέα πιθαμαὶς τὸ πλάτος του μετρᾶται,
εἶναι δὲ σὰν μυλόπετρα πᾶς λίθος καὶ ὁρᾶται·
πέντε δὲ πάλιν πιθαμαὶς τὸ χόντρος ὁ καθένας,
τοὺς κύτταζα καὶ ἔχασα καὶ τὴν φωνὴν καὶ φρένας·
ὡσὰν κ᾽ ἐμένα ἄνθρωποι πεντὲξ νὰ ξαπλωθοῦσι
ἀπάνω του ὅλοι ἐκεῖ χωρὶς ἄλλο χωροῦσι·
καὶ ὡς τριάντα πιθαμαὶς τὸ γύρω κάθε λίθος,
μὲ τώλεγαν καὶ ἔλεγα ὅτι πῶς εἶναι μῦθος·
ὅτι διήγημα ἐκεῖ εἶναι αὐτὴ ἡ στήλη,
καὶ τὴν ἀκοῦς καὶ τὴν θωρεῖς στοῦ καθενὸς τὰ χείλη.
Ἀτός μου τοὺς ἐμέτρησα μὲ ἔπαινον μεγάλον
ἐκείνων τῶν κτιτόρων της τῶν θείων, ὄχι ἄλλων,
ἐκείνων τῶν ἡρώων της, τῶν ἀληθῶν ἀνθρώπων,
τῶν ἀσεβῶν, ἀλλ᾽ εὐσεβῶν κατὰ ψυχὴν καὶ τρόπον.
Ὅθεν ὁ κτίστης μας Θεὸς αὐτοὺς ἐβοηθοῦσε,
τέτοιαις πέτραις σήκονε, καὶ ταὶς οἰκοδομοῦσε·
καὶ συνεργεῖ κ᾽ εὐφραίνεται Θεὸς ἐπ᾽ ἀληθείας,
εἰς τῶν ἀνθρώπων τῶν καλῶν τὰς τέχνας καὶ σοφίας·
τὰ ἔργ᾽ αὐτῶν τὰ εὐλογεῖ καὶ τοὺς τὰ στερεόνει
καὶ τοὺς σοφίζει καὶ αὐτοὺς καὶ τοὺς ἐνδυναμόνει.
Καὶ εἶν᾽ ἐπάνω πανωταὶς πέτραις θηριακωμέναις
εἰς τόσον ὕψος ὑψηλά, κι ὅλαις πελεκημέναις
ὡσὰν νὰ εἶναι κόσκινα ἕνα ἀπάνω τ᾽ ἄλλο,
ὡσὰν κεφαλοτύρια, πρᾶγμα πολλὰ μεγάλο.
Δὲν εἶναι δὲ καὶ μοναχή, ὑπὲρ τὰς δέκα εἶναι,
αὐτὸ κάνει τὸν θεατὴν φρῖξαι καὶ ἐκπλαγῆναι,
ὅτι δὲν εἶναι μόνον μιά, πλειὸ παρὰ δέκα εἶναι,

The seven wonders of the ancient world.
Indeed the Samian column should be named
And be regarded as the eighth in line.
You can see it from afar, two hours' away;
It calls out to you to go and view it.
Now listen in amazement and rejoice,
And tell it to the world: each column drum
Does measure eight or nine handspans in width;
Each drum resembles thus a millstone.
In thickness too each measures five handspans.
As I looked on, I lost my voice and mind.
Five men or six like me could spread themselves
Upon it and everyone could fit there.
When I was told each measures thirty handspans
In circumference, I thought it was a myth;
I thought this column was a fancy tale,
One that you see and hear on everybody's lips.
I measured them myself and greatly praised
The blessed men who built it—not the others,
Those so-called heroes, but the real men,
Ungodly men but sound in soul and ways.
And so our God, a builder, helped these men
To raise such boulders and to build with them.
Our God cooperates, delighting in
The skills and wisdom righteous men display.
He blesses all their works and makes them firm,
While granting people wisdom, will and strength.
Big as beasts, the stones are in a pile that
Reaches high, so high, and all are chiselled.
They resemble drum sieves in a pile
Or blocks of cheese, a thing immense indeed.
There is not one but more than ten of these,
Which makes the viewer stand in shock and awe,
That there is not only one but more than ten.

αὐτὴ ὅμως δυνήθηκεν ἕως τοῦ νῦν σταθῆναι,
θέαμα νἆναι θαυμαστὸ, σάλπιγξ καὶ τῆς ἀνδρείας
τῶν πάλαι προπατόρων μας, ἀλλὰ καὶ τῆς σοφίας·
καθὼς εἰς τὸ Βυζάντιον ἡ στήλη ἡ σκασμένη
εἶναι ἀπάνω στὸ τζαρσί, ἡ σιδηροδεμένη,
κ' ἡ ἄλλη ἡ μονόλιθος στήλη ἡ ξακουσμένη
εἰς τέσσερα ποδάρια προύντζινα ἱσταμένη·
κήρυκες μεγαλόφωνοι ἡ μὲν Θεοδοσίου,
ἡ δὲ τοῦ Κωνσταντίνου μας ἐκείνου τοῦ ἁγίου,
ἐκείνων τῶν ἡρωϊκῶν μεγάλων βασιλέων,
ἐκείνων τῶν βασιλικῶν ἡρώων καὶ ἐνθέων·
λείψανα τῆς προχθεσινῆς δικῆς μας ἐξουσίας,
ἀγάλματα τῆς κραταιᾶς ἐκείνης βασιλείας,
στολίσματα τοῦ ἱεροῦ βασιλικοῦ μας θρόνου,
ὑπὸ τοῦ χρόνου ἄφθαρτα καὶ τοῦ παμφθόρου φθόνου·
γιατὶ τ' ἄλλα τ' ἀφάνισε τοῦ φθόνου ἡ πανώλης,
πράγματ' ἀξιοθέατα τῆς βασιλίσσης Πόλης·
καὶ ὡς καθὼς στὴν Αἴγυπτον εἶναι οἱ πυραμίδες
καὶ ὀβελίσκοι οἱ ψηλοί, ἂν καὶ νὰ μὴ τοὺς εἶδες,
ἀφ' ὧν δυὸ τρεῖς ἐσήκωσαν, τοὺς πῆγαν εἰς τὴν Ῥώμην
οἱ παλαιοί της βασιλεῖς μὲ λαμπροτάτην γνώμην.

. . . .

Μέσα εἰς ἕνα σπήλαιον ἀμμὴ πολλὰ μεγάλο
θαρρῶ δὲν εἶναι σὰν αὐτὸ στὴν Σάμον ὅλην ἄλλο·
ὅτι, νὰ μὲ πιστεύσετε, τῆς Βαλεδὲς τὸ χάνι
τὸ εἰς Κωνσταντινούπολιν αὐτὸ μέσα τὸ βάνει·
ἂν ἦτον ὑψηλότερο καὶ φωτεινὸ, περνοῦσε
κεῖνο τὸ μωραΐτικο καὶ μέσα τὸ χωροῦσε,
κ' ἐκεῖνο τοῦ Ὁμήρου δέ, ὁποῦ ἐκατοικοῦσε
ὁ κύκλωψ ὁ Πολύφημος καὶ πρόβατα βοσκοῦσε,
καὶ ὁ μαργέλος Ὀδυσσεὺς μὲ τὸ γλυκὸ κρασάκι
τὸν μαῦρον τὸν ἐτύφλωσεν, ὁποὖχε στὸ τλουμάκι.
Αὐτὸ εὑρίσκεται κοντὰ στὸ κάστρο ὁποῦ εἶπα,
καὶ ἔχει ἔμπασμα μικρὸ καὶ φαίνεται σὰν τρῦπα·

Yet this has managed still to stand erect,
A sight beyond belief, an emblem of
The fortitude and wisdom our forebears.
It is like the cracked column in Byzantium
Inside the forum, fixed with metal hoops,
Or that famous monolithic column
Erected on a set of four bronze legs,
Grand emblems—the latter of Theodosius,
The former of our Saint Constantine,
Two mighty and heroic emperors,
Two heroes, imperial and divine.
They are relics of our power in the past,
Statues from an empire strong and vast,
Embellishments of our royal sacred throne,
Unscathed by time or noxious envy,
Which, like a plague, did cause to disappear
The City's other splendid monuments.
This was the case with Egypt's pyramids
And obelisks, which you have never seen.
Past emperors took two or three of these,
Carrying them off to Rome in stately style.
. . . .
There is a cave that is extremely large,
The biggest one I think that Samos has,
So huge, believe me, that the Valide Han
In Constantinople would fit inside.
If it were higher and brighter, it would
Surpass that cave in the Peloponnese,
Or the one in Homer where the Cyclops
Polyphemus lived and tended his sheep,
That wretched one whom wily Odysseus
Blinded with red wine kept in his wineskin.
This cave is near the temple that I mentioned
And has a tiny entrance, like a hole.

εἰς τοῦτο μέσα τὸ λοιπὸν εἶν' ἐκκλησία μία,
ἔξω στὸ ἔμπασμ' ἄλλη μιὰ κ' εἶναι ἡ Παναγία,
καὶ λέγεται Σπηλιανὴ πρεπόντως Παναγία,
ἡ χάρις της καὶ ἡ εὐχὴ σκέπη μας σωτηρία.
Εἶναι δὲ ἡ εἰκόνα της ἀρχαία καὶ πετρίνη,
τὸ μάκρος δύο σπιθαμαὶς, ἡ πέτρα δὲ κοκκίνη·
ὄπισθεν δὲ τοῦ βήματος, μέσα εἰσὲ λακκάκι,
βρύει κ' εὑρίσκεται ἐκεῖ γλυκύτατο νεράκι·
εἰς ἄλλο μέρος πάλιν δὲ εἶναι καὶ δυὸ σκαμμέναις
στέρναις ἀπὸ τὸ παλαιό, μεγάλαις, γεμισμέναις
ἀπ' τὰ νεροσταλάμματα ὁποῦ ἐκεῖ σταλάζει
τὸ μέγα σπήλαιον αὐτὸ ὁλοχρονὶς καὶ στάζει·
πράγματα ὁποῦ μ' ἔκαμαν αὐταὶς κ' ἡ ἐκκλησία
καὶ νὰ δοξάσω τὸν Θεὸν καὶ νὰ 'φρανθῇ καρδία.
Μέσα ἐμπαίνοντας ἐγώ, οἱ μετ' ἐμοῦ κρατοῦσαν
μίαν λαμπάδα ὁ καθεὶς, καὶ ἐπεριπατοῦσαν·
κ' ἔφθασα εἰς ταὶς ἄκραις του, περίεργος ὡς ὄντας,
τὴν φυσικήν μου ὄρεξιν σωστὰ πληροφορῶντας·
φύσει γὰρ πάντες ἄνθρωποι, φησὶν ὁ Σταγειρίτης,
ὀρέγονται νὰ ξεύρουσι, καὶ νέος καὶ πρεσβύτης.
Οἱ Σάμιοι γιὰ τὸ πολὺ τὸ βάθος καὶ σκοτίδι
τρέμουν νὰ τὸ γυρίσουσι, σὰ νᾶναι μέσα φίδι·
καὶ λέγουν πὼς τὸ σπήλαιον δὲν ἔχει ἄκρην, τέλος,
καὶ εἶναι μία καὶ αὐτὸ μυθολογία, γέλως.
Ἡ Ἄντρος νῆσος λέγεται πὼς καὶ ἐκείνη ἔχει,
γιὰ τοῦτο Ἄντρος λέγεται, πολλὰ γὰρ περιέχει·
τέτοια ὅμως σπήλαια δὲν εἶναι λογιάζω
οὐδὲ στὴν Ἄντρον, οὐδ' ἀλλοῦ, λογιάζω καὶ σᾶς τάζω.
Ἐδῶ, ἀφέντη μου, θωρεῖς καὶ τὸ τοῦ Πυθαγόρα
τοῦ περιφήμου σπήλαιον, καὶ τότε δὲ καὶ τώρα,
ὁποῦ ἐκ παραδόσεως ἔχουσιν οἱ Σαμιῶται
πὼς εἰς αὐτὸ ἀσκήτευεν ὁ Πυθαγόρας τότε·
καὶ ἡ συνείδησις εὐθὺς ἐκεῖ θέλει σε πλήξῃ,
καὶ πόσον ἁγιώτερος εἶναι σὲ θέλει δείξῃ

Inside this cave a church exists, and by
The entrance there is yet another church,
One rightly called the Virgin of the Caves,
Who shields and saves us by her prayers and grace.
Her icon is quite old and made of stone,
The stone is red and spans two palms in length.
Behind the altar, in a little pit,
There is some flowing water, fresh and sweet.
And in another place there are two cisterns
Dug from ancient times, enormous ones,
Both filled from drops of water trickling down
Throughout the year inside the spacious cave.
The church and these two cisterns led me to
Give praise to God and made my heart rejoice.
I went inside this cave and those with me
Were holding each a candle as they walked.
Being curious, I reached the very end,
Fulfilling thus my natural desire.
As Aristotle said, all people young
And old by nature have the urge to know.
Its depth and darkness scare the locals, who
Are loath to walk right in, as if there lurked
A snake; they say it has no edge or end,
But that is just a myth that makes one laugh.
They say that Andros too has many caves,
And for this very reason bears this name.
But even there, or anywhere for sure,
You may not chance upon a cave like this.
Here too, my prince, you may behold the cave
Of Pythagoras, renowned both then and now,
Which Samian tradition claims to be
The actual cave where the ascetic used to live.
And there the realization strikes at once
How much greater than you in holiness

ὁ Ἕλληνας φιλόσοφος αὐτὸς ἀπὸ ἐσένα,
καὶ ἐν ταὐτῷ ἀπὸ ἐμὲ τὸν ὀκνηρὸν ἐμένα·
ὁποῦ τὸν κόσμον καὶ ἡμεῖς δὲν τὸν ἀπαρατοῦμεν
νὰ πᾶμε ν' ἀσκητεύσωμεν, στὰ σπήλαια νὰ μποῦμεν.
....

Κι ἄν ἀνασταίνουνταν αὐτὸς ὁ Πυθαγόρας τώρα,
τοῦ πρώην κόσμου ὁ νουνός, δὲν ζοῦσε μίαν ὥρα·
καί, ἄν ἐζοῦσε, παρευθὺς δὲν ἤθελε μιλήσῃ,
ἤθελε χάσῃ τὴν φωνήν, τὸ στόμα του νὰ κλείσῃ·
ἤθελε μείνῃ ἄλαλος, βουβὸς δεκαετίαν,
ὄχι καθὼς ἐδίδασκε σιγὴν πενταετίαν.
Οἱ τρεῖς οἱ φίλοι τοῦ Ἰώβ, βλέποντες πληγωμένον
αὐτὸν τὸν φίλον τους Ἰὼβ κ' ἔτζι καταστημένον,
ἑπτὰ μέραις δὲν σύντυχαν, ἐδέθηκεν ἡ γλῶσσα,
καὶ ἡ φωνή τους πιάσθηκεν εἰς τὰ κακὰ τὰ τόσα.
Ὁ Πυθαγόρας βλέποντας τὸν κόσμον χαλασμένον,
διεφθαρμένον πανταχοῦ, κ' ἔτζι καταντημένον,
ὑπόθεσις νὰ βουβαθῇ, νὰ τοῦ δεθῇ ἡ γλῶσσα,
εἰς τὰ μεγάλα καὶ φρικτὰ κακὰ τοῦ κόσμου τόσα.

This Greek philosopher appears to be,
Greater than me as well, idle as I am.
For we would never abandon the world
And go to live as hermits in a cave.
. . . .
And if Pythagoras were to return,
Patron of the past, he would not last an hour.
And if he did, he would not speak at all.
He would lose his voice and shut his mouth,
Remaining dumb and speechless for a decade,
Beyond the five-year silence that he taught.
When Job's three friends beheld his plight
And saw their friend in such a wretched state,
Seven days they did not meet; their tongue was tied,
Their voice was lost, before his many woes.
And if Pythagoras could see how spoiled
And utterly corrupt the world has grown,
He too would go dumb and lose his voice,
Before the world's so many dreadful woes.

ΛΟΓΟΙ ΠΑΝΗΓΥΡΙΚΟΙ/
PANEGYRICS

Κανὼν περιεκτικὸς πολλῶν ἐξαιρέτων πραγμάτων[*]

ΩΔΗ α΄ «Ἀνοίξω τὸ στόμα μου»[**]

Ἀνοίξω τὸ στόμα μου, καὶ διηγήσομαι πάμπολλα ἐξαίρετα πράγματα. Δεῦτε ἀκούσατε, δεῦτε ἄρχοντες, δεῦτε, πραγματευτάδες, δεῦτε καὶ οἱ πλούσιοι, δεῦτε καὶ πένητες.

Κρασὶ Σκοπελίτικο, κουμανταριὰ ἡ Κυπριώτικη, μοσχάτο Σαμιώτικο, καὶ μερικὰ τῆς Φραγγιᾶς. Δάντζκας βοῦτκαις δὲ, καὶ Βλαχομπογδανίας, ροσόλια Κορφιάτικα, ἐκλεκτὰ πράγματα.

Γαρόφαλα Χιώτικα, καὶ ἡ μαστίχη καὶ μύγδαλα, μῆλα τὰ Μπογδάνικα, κεράσια τῶν Γραβνῶν, Βλαχιᾶς βύσσινα, οἱ ραζακαῖς σταφίδες, καὶ σῦκα τῆς Σμύρνης δέ, ἐκλεκτὰ πράγματα.

Πόλης τὰ ροδάκινα, Ὄρους Σινᾶ τὰ ἀπίδια, τὰ κίτρα τὰ Χιώτικα καὶ τὰ Ἀξιώτικα, καὶ τὰ Κώτικα ἐκεῖνα τὰ καρπούζια, πεπόνια τὰ Βόδινα, ἐκλεκτὰ πράγματα.

Τῆς Προύσας τὰ κάστανα, τοῦ Χαλεπιοῦ τὰ φιστίκια, τῆς Κίος τὰ ρόδια, τὰ καϊσιὰ Δαμασκοῦ, καὶ δαμάσκηνα, Μάλτας τὰ πορτοκάλια, καὶ τοῦ Ῥαχιτίου δέ, ἐκλεκτὰ πράγματα.

[*] The text is based on the original publication in *Λόγοι πανηγυρικοί* (1778), pp. 107–16. For the most part I have retained the original spelling; proper nouns have been capitalized and punctuation marks adjusted for the sake of clarity.

[**] The phrase at the head of each ode comes from the Akathist Hymn and corresponds to the first few words of the *eirmos*, an introductory stanza serving as a thematic link and setting the melody and meter for each ode. Following the Akathist Hymn's tradition, Dapontes's Canon omits the second ode.

Canon of Hymns Containing Many Exceptional Things*

ODE I "I shall open my mouth"

I shall open my mouth and speak of many exceptional things. Come forth and listen magistrates and merchants, come forth and listen, be you rich or poor.

Wine of the isle of Skopelos, commandaria from Cyprus, Samian muscat and some spirits from France; the vodka of Danzig, Wallachia and Moldavia, and the rosolios of Corfu are all such exquisite things.

The cloves of Chios, its mastic and almonds; the apples of Moldavia, cherries of Grevena, morellos of Wallachia, and Smyrna sultanas and figs are all such exquisite things.

The peaches of Constantinople, pears of Mount Sinai, citrons of Chios and Naxos, the watermelons of Kos, and melons of Vodena are all such exquisite things.

Bursa's chestnuts, Aleppo's pistachios and Kios's pomegranates; apricots and damsons of Damascus, oranges of Malta and Rosetta are all such exquisite things.

* The index and glossary in Savvidis 1991a: 95–148 were particularly helpful in the translation of this text.

ΩΔΗ γ΄ «Τοὺς σοὺς ὑμνολόγους»

Παντζέχρι φιδιοῦ καὶ σκαντζοχοίρου, ὁ μπάλσαμος Μέκας καὶ
κουρμᾶς, ὁ μόσχος ὁ Κινέζικος, θηριακὴ Βενέτικη, Χιώτικο
γιασουμόλαδο, ὄντως ἐξαίρετα πράγματα.

Ἐγγλέζικη ζάχαρη καὶ στάμπα, μπαρούτι καὶ ναύτης δὲ καὶ ναῦς,
καὶ ὥρα καὶ καθρέπτης δέ, καὶ τὰ σαλιὰ τῆς Ἄγκυρας, ὁμοῦ καὶ τὰ
τεφτίκια, ὄντως ἐξαίρετα πράγματα.

Τριαντάφυλλα Φράντζας καὶ ἀντζόγαις, καὶ κάππαρι, καὶ Μυτιληνιαῖς
μυζίθραις, καὶ κυδώνια, τῆς Ἀδριανουπόλεως, καὶ οἱ ἐλιαῖς τῆς Κρήτης
δέ, ὄντως ἐξαίρετα πράγματα.

Τὰ βόδια τὰ τῆς Μπογδανίας, τὰ πρόβατα τῆς Καραμανιᾶς, Βλαχιᾶς τὰ
κασκαβάλια, χαβγιάρι Βιδυνίσιο, τζίγαις, μουροῦναις Δούναβι, ὄντως
ἐξαίρετα πράγματα.

Τῆς Αἴνου καὶ τοῦ Μεσολογγίου τὰ ψάρια, οἱ τζίροι τ᾽ Ἀριτζιοῦ, ξιφιὸς
δὲ ὁ Πολίτικος, ξυρίχι Ἀζακίσιο, καὶ παστουρμᾶς Καισάρειας, ὄντως
ἐξαίρετα πράγματα.

ODE III "Those who sing hymns of praise to you"

Snake stones and porcupine bezoars, Mecca's balsam and dates, China's musk, Venetian treacle, and Chian jasmine oil are really exceptional things.

England's sugar and typography, its gunpowder, sailors and ships, and mirrors and clocks; the camlets of Ankara, as well as its mohair, are really exceptional things.

French roses, anchovies, and capers; the myzithra of Mytilene, quinces of Adrianople and olives of Crete are really exceptional things.

The oxen of Moldavia, sheep of Karaman, Wallachian kashkaval and the caviar of Vidin, and the Danube's sturgeons and sterlets are really exceptional things.

Fish of Aenus and Messolonghi, dried mackerel of Aretsou; the swordfish of Constantinople, sturgeons of Azov, and seasoned beef of Kayseri are really exceptional things.

ΩΔΗ δ΄ «Ὁ καθήμενος ἐν δόξῃ»

Τὰ πετράδια Ἰνδίας, κεχριμπάρι τὸ Λέχικο, ὁ ἄνθραξ ὁ λίθος, τὸ
μαργαριτάρι Χουρμούζιον, τὰ φαρφουρία, τὰ τζάγια, τὰ ῥαβέντια καὶ
μετάξια Κίνας, ἐξαίσια πράγματα.

Τὰ Βενέτικα φλωρία, Χαμπεσίας τὸ μάλαμα, Ἰσπανῶν σιβίλλια, τὸ
τῆς Μοσχοβίας μπαλούκτισι, τῆς Σαρδηνίας κοράλλι, καὶ τὰ μέταλλα
Τραπεζοῦντος δέ, ὄντως ἐξαίσια πράγματα.

Ὁ καφὲς τοῦ Γεμενίου, τὸ λινάρι τὸ Φιούμι δέ, Μπαρμπαριᾶς τὰ φέσια,
Κίνας καὶ Σερρῶν τὰ βαμπάκια, οἱ βισταλόγγαις τῆς Ῥώμης, καὶ τῆς
Βέρρροιας τὰ προσόψια, ὄντως ἐξαίσια πράγματα.

Μολδοβίας καὶ Βλαχίας μελισσῶν τὸ πολύγονον, καὶ τὸ πολύ ἄλας,
τὸ Ταραμπουλούσι σαπούνιον, Λαοδικείας τουτοῦνι, καὶ τοξάρια τὰ
Τατάρικα, ὄντως ἐξαίσια πράγματα.

Οἱ Πολίτκαις ἀγγηνάραις, τ᾽ Ἁγιορείτκα λεφτόκαρα, Ταμιατιοῦ τὸ
ῥίζι, τὰ τοῦ Μπρασοβοῦ παξιμάδια, καὶ τῆς Βλαχιᾶς τὰ καϊμάκια καὶ τ᾽
ἀγγούρια τὰ τῆς Βλάγγας δέ, ὄντως ἐξαίσια πράγματα.

ODE IV "He who sits in glory"

Indian diamonds, Polish amber, garnet gemstones, and pearls from
the Strait of Hormuz; the porcelain of China, its teas, rhubarb, and
silk are truly excellent things.

Venetian florins, Abyssinian gold, and silver coins of Spain; the
mammoth ivory of Moscow, corals of Sardinia, and minerals of
Trebizond are truly excellent things.

Coffee from Yemen, flax from Fayum and fezzes from the Barbary
Coast; the cotton of China and Serres, telescopes of Rome and
towels of Veroia are truly excellent things.

The abundance of bees and stores of salt in Moldavia and Wallachia;
Tripolitan soap, Latakia tobacco, and the Tatars' arrows and bows
are truly excellent things.

The artichokes of Constantinople, hazelnuts of Mount Athos,
Damietta's rice, and Braşov's rusks; Wallachian cream, and the
cucumbers from Vlanga are truly excellent things.

ΩΔΗ ε΄ «Ἐξέστη τὰ σύμπαντα»

Εἰκόνες Μοσχόβικαις, σταυροὶ Ἁγιορήτικοι, λάδανος τῆς Κύπρου καὶ τῆς Κρήτης, τὸ πρινοκοῦκκι τὸ Μωραΐτικο, πράσινο κηρὶ τῆς Μπογδανιᾶς, καὶ γοῦναις Μοσχόβικαις, εὐμορφώτατα πράγματα.

Λάδι τὸ Κορφιάτικο, σταφίδες Ζακυνθήσιαις, κρόκκος Ἁγιορήτικος καὶ βρύσες, τ᾽ Ἁγιοταφήτικα ροδοστάματα, Χίου τὰ ἀνθόνερα ὁμοῦ, Μπάστρας τὸ ἐντερσαΐ, εὐμορφώτατα πράγματα.

Ὀρτύκια Μανιάτικα, σουτζοῦκι τὸ Γριππιώτικο, τὸ μέλι Ἀθήνας καὶ Σπανίας, οἱ Σκοπελίτικαις οἱ μουστόπιταις, τὸ πιαζεντὶ τῆς Βενετιᾶς, τ᾽ Ἀμανιοῦ τὸ βούτυρο, εὐμορφώτατα πράγματα.

Τουνίναις οἱ Χιώτικαις, ὄρκυνοι οἱ Γριππιώτικοι, Βενετιᾶς σουπιαῖς, Σμύρνης καρίδες, καὶ καραβίδες Βλαχομπογδάνικαις, οἱ Μαρμαρινοὶ δὲ οἱ κολοί, καὶ χέλυα Γιαννιώτικα, εὐμορφώτατα πράγματα.

Ῥώσων μοσχοπόντικα, Νήσων τὰ μοσχοχτάποδα, Κούταλης καβούρια, καὶ τῆς Πόλης στρίδια καὶ χτένια καὶ αὐγοτάραχα, χιοβάδες στὰ Τούσλα, κ᾽ Ἐρυθρᾶς Θαλάσσης σεδέφια, εὐμορφώτατα πράγματα.

ODE V "The universe was amazed"

The icons of Moscow and crosses of Athos, ladanum of Cyprus
and Crete; kermes dye from the Peloponnese, Moscow's furs, and
Moldavian green wax are all magnificent things.

Oil of Corfu, currants of Zante, Mount Athos saffron and springs;
rose water from the Holy Sepulchre, orange blossom water from
Chios and Basra's sweet sultans are all magnificent things.

Mani quails, Euboean *sucuk*, honey from Athens and Spain; the
must pies of Skopelos, Venetian *piacentino*, and butter from the milk
of Amman are all magnificent things.

Little tunny of Chios, bluefin tuna of Euboea, Venetian cuttlefish
and Smyrna's prawns; the crayfish of Moldavia and Wallachia, eels of
Ioannina and mackerel from the Sea of Marmara are all magnificent
things.

The Russians' otter pelts, the islands' musky octopus, Koutali's crabs
and Constantinople's oysters, scallops and roe; the cockles of Tuzla,
and the Red Sea's mother-of-pearl are all magnificent things.

ΩΔΗ στ´ «Τὴν θείαν ταύτην»

Νήσων τινῶν πετροκόσσυφοι, κανάρια ὁμοῦ τὰ Βενέτικα, τὰ
γραφοφόρα δὲ τοῦ Μπαγδατιοῦ περιστέρια, τῇ ἀληθείᾳ πράγματα
ἀξιόλογα.

Σκυλιὰ Σαμψώνια τὰ Νέμτζικα, σκυλιὰ δὲ καὶ γεράκια τὰ Βλάχικα
καὶ τὰ Μπογδάνικα, διὰ κυνῆγι τὰ χρήσιμα, τῇ ἀληθείᾳ πράγματα
ἀξιόλογα.

Τὰ πορφυρᾶ Χίου μάρμαρα, τῆς Κίνας καὶ Περσίας ὑφάσματα, καὶ
τῆς Ἰνδίας δὲ καὶ Μαδαγάσκαρ τ᾽ ἀρώματα, τῇ ἀληθείᾳ πράγματα
ἀξιόλογα.

Κῶς καὶ Βοστίτζας ὁ πλάτανος, τῆς Θάσου ἐλαιὼν ὁ θαλάσσιος, τὰ
περιβόλια τοῦ Παρισιοῦ καὶ παλάτια, τῇ ἀληθείᾳ πράγματα ἀξιόλογα.

Ὀλύμπων ὕψος καὶ Ἄθωνος, ὁ κάμπος Θετταλίας καὶ Τόμπριζας, καὶ ἡ
τῆς Βύζαντος τοποθεσία καὶ αὔξησις, τῇ ἀληθείᾳ πράγματα ἀξιόλογα.

ODE VI "This divine [feast]"

Island rock thrushes, Venetian canaries, and the carrier pigeons of Baghdad are truly admirable things.

German dogs, and the falcons and hounds from Wallachia and Moldavia, fit for hunting, are truly admirable things.

The red marble of Chios, Chinese and Persian textiles, and the spices of India and Madagascar are truly admirable things.

The plane tree in Vostitsa and Kos, olive groves on Thasian shores, and Paris's palaces and parks are truly admirable things.

The peaks of Athos and Olympus, Thessalian plains and the Dobruja plateau, the ambience and abundance of Bizye are truly admirable things.

ΩΔΗ ζ΄ «Οὐκ ἐλάτρευσαν»

Ὁ Παράδεισος, ὁ τάφος τοῦ Κυρίου μου, χιτών, μανδήλιον,
Ξηροποτάμου Μονῆς τὸ Ξύλον τὸ τίμιον, Ἐσθὴς καὶ Ζώνη τε τῆς
Κυρίας μου, τὸ σῶμα τοῦ Σπυρίδωνος, θέας ἄξια τῷ ὄντι.

Τὸ Ποτήριον, μεθ᾽ οὗ ὁ Χριστὸς ἔπιε στὸν Δεῖπνον τὸν μυστικὸν μετὰ
καὶ τῶν Μαθητῶν, τὸ κολοκυθένιον, ὅπερ εἰς τὸ Τζαοὺς Μοναστήριον
Θεσσαλονίκης σώζεται, θέας ἄξια τῷ ὄντι.

Τὰ τοῦ Ἄθωνος εἴκοσι μοναστήρια, καὶ οἱ εἰκόνες οἱ τρεῖς τοῦ
Ἀποστόλου Λουκᾶ,
Ἁγία Σοφία τε κ᾽ ἡ αὐτῆς τράπεζα, καὶ ἡ παρ᾽ ἐμοὶ εἰκὼν τῆς Παναγίας
μου, θέας ἄξια τῷ ὄντι.

Τὰ Μετέωρα ἐκεῖνα μοναστήρια, τὸ ἐν τῷ Στήρει δὲ τῷ τῆς Φωκίδος
Λουκᾶ, Ναὸς ὁ τῆς Πάρου δὲ ὁ ἑκατόμπυλος, κι ὁ Μπογδάνικος κι ὁ
Βλάχικος οἱ σκαλιστοί, θέας ἄξια τῷ ὄντι.

Σαραντάριον, Σινᾶ, Θαβὼρ καὶ Ἀραράτ, τὸ Μέγα Σπήλαιον, Μορέως
τὸ ἱερόν, κ᾽ ἐκεῖνο τῆς Πάτμου δέ, τὸ Εὐαγγέλιον ἔνθα ἔγραψεν ὁ φίλος
καὶ Ἀπόστολος, θέας ἄξια τῷ ὄντι.

Τὸ Κατάστενο τῆς Πόλεως, οἱ τέσσαρες οἱ ποταμοὶ τῆς Ἐδέμ, ἡ
Ζωοδόχος Πηγή, τὸ ὕδωρ τοῦ Σιλωάμ, ὁ Ἰορδάνης τε καὶ ὁ Δούναβις
καὶ ἡ Νεκρὰ ἡ Θάλασσα, θέας ἄξια τῷ ὄντι.

ODE VII "They did not worship [creation but the Creator]"

Paradise, the tomb of my Lord, His tunic and shroud; the fragment of the True Cross in the Monastery of Xeropotamos; my Lady's girdle and gown, and the relics of Saint Spyridon are truly worth beholding.

The calabash cup from which Christ drunk with His disciples at the Last Supper, surviving in Vlatadon, a monastery in Thessalonike is truly worth beholding.

The twenty monasteries of Mount Athos, the three icons of Saint Luke, the Church of Hagia Sophia, its altar too, and my own icon of the Mother of God are truly worth beholding.

The monasteries of Meteora, that of Luke in Steiri of Phocis, the hundred-gate church on the island of Paros, and the wood carvings on the churches in Moldavia and Wallachia are truly worth beholding.

The Sarindar Monastery, Mount Sinai, Tabor, and Ararat; the Great Cave Monastery in the Peloponnese, and the one on Patmos, where John the Apostle whom Jesus loved, wrote the Book of Revelation, are truly worth beholding.

The Bosporus of Constantinople and four rivers of Eden; the Fountain of Life and Pool of Siloam; the Jordan, the Danube, and the Dead Sea are truly worth beholding.

ΩΔΗ η΄ «Παῖδας εὐαγεῖς»

Ἡ Κόλτζα ἡ ἐν Βουκουρεστίῳ, Σὰν Μάρκου τῆς Βενετίας τὸ
καμπαναριό καὶ τὸ ὡρολόγιον, καὶ τοῦ κατὰ Κίοβον Πετζέρσκη, καὶ τὰ
λείψανα τὰ διακόσια, ἀλλὰ καὶ ἡ ἐν τῇ Πετρουπόλει ἐκείνη καμπάνα,
ἄξια θεωρίας.

Τοῦ Πέτρου Ναὸς ὁ ἐν τῇ Ρώμῃ, Τριάδος δὲ τὸ Πετζέρσκη, ὅπερ
εἴπομεν, καὶ ὁ εἰς Πετρούπολιν, ἐν ᾧ ἐστὶ, λέγουσι τὸ τοῦ Λουκᾶ
εἰκόνισμα τῆς Παναγίας μου, πρὸς τούτοις ἐκεῖνος, ἐν ᾧ τάφοι οἱ τῶν
Βασιλέων, ἄξια θεωρίας.

Μωάμεθ τὸ μνῆμα καὶ οἱ μαῦροι Λιβύης καὶ ἡ ἀμμώδης της ἡ ἔρημος,
Κυζίκου, Κασσάνδρας τε οἱ λαιμοὶ καὶ Ἄθωνος, ἡ τῆς Εὐρώπης γέφυρα
ἐπὶ τὴν Εὔριππον, τῆς Κίνας τὸ τεῖχος καὶ Τρῳάδος, τὰ λουτρὰ τῆς
Προύσας, ἄξια θεωρίας.

Τῆς Πόλης τζαμιὰ καὶ ἡ κολώνα, ὁ πύργος ὁ φαρφουρένιος ὁ Κινέζικος
καὶ ὁ ἐν Κρεμώνῃ δέ, τῆς Ἄντρου τὰ σπήλαια, τῆς Κίνας τὰ γεφύρια,
καὶ τὸ Βενέτικο, τῆς Ἀδριανουπόλεως ἔτι καὶ τῶν Τζεκμετζέδων, ἄξια
θεωρίας.

Ἡ Αἴτνη, ἡ Χάρυβδις, ἡ Σκύλλα, τοῦ Νείλου πλημμύρα καὶ
καταρράκται καὶ πηγαί, Εὐρίππου, Εὐφράτου τε, Τίγριδος παλίρροιαι,
τοῦ Ἀμστερδὰμ ἡ θάλασσα, τὸ Κιλιμπουράνιον, ὁ λιμὴν ἐκεῖνος τῆς
Ἀγκῶνος, Μοίριδος ἡ λίμνη, ἄξια θεωρίας.

Τὸ ἄπουν πουλὶ τὸ τῆς Ἰνδίας, ὁ φοίνιξ τῆς Ἀραβίας ὁ μονογενής,
ταώς, παπαγάλλος τε, λέων, στρουθοκάμηλος, πάνθηρ, κακοῦμι,
πάρδαλις, τίγρις, μονόκερως, ἐλέφας, κροκόδειλος, φοράδες οἱ τῆς
Ἀραβίας, ἄξια θεωρίας.

ODE VIII "Pious youth"

The Coltea hospital in Bucharest, the campanile and clock tower of Saint Mark's in Venice; the belfry of the Kiev Cave Monastery, its two hundred relics and the bell tower in Saint Petersburg are worth observing.

Saint Peter's in Rome, the Holy Trinity of Pechersk, the church in Saint Petersburg containing, as they say, the icon of Our Lady by Saint Luke, and that church with the tombs of the Tsars are worth observing.

The tomb of Muhammad, Libya's blacks and desert dunes; the peninsulas of Cyzicus, Kassandra and Mount Athos; the bridge across Euripus to get across to Europe; Bursa's baths and the walls of China and Troy are worth observing.

The mosques and obelisk in Constantinople, the porcelain tower of China and torazzo of Cremona; the caves of Andros, the bridges of China, Venice, and Adrianople, as well as those of Çekmece, are worth observing.

Mount Etna, Scylla, and Charybdis; the Nile's floods, waterfalls, and springs; the tides of Tigris, Euripus and Euphrates, and the sea of Amsterdam; Kinburn cape, Ancona port, and Lake Moeris are worth observing.

The swift of India, the self-born phoenix of Arabia, the peacock, parrot, ostrich, lion, panther, leopard and stoat; the tiger, unicorn, elephant and crocodile, and mares of the Arabian world are worth observing.

ΩΔΗ θ΄ «Ἅπας γηγενὴς»

Ἡ Πίστις ἡμῶν, Τουρκῶν τὸ φιλόξενον, κούρτη Φραντζέζικη, Ἐνετῶν
εὐγένεια, τῶν Ἰουδαίων δὲ ἡ ὁμόνοια, τὰ Μπρουσσικὰ στρατεύματα,
ἡ τῶν Σκυθῶν τοξική, τῶν Ἰγκλέζων δὲ τὸ ναυτιλώτατον, Ἰσπανῶν τὸ
εὐθές, ἀξιάγαστα.

Ῥωμαίων ὁ νοῦς, Φραγγῶν τὸ καλλίτεχνον καὶ πολυμήχανον, Ἀλβανῶν
τὸ εὔψυχον, Ἠπειρωτῶν τε τὸ σωφρονέστατον, τῶν Ῥώσσων ἡ
εὐσέβεια, καὶ ὁ νῦν πόλεμος, τῶν Ἰβήρων τὸ ἐλευθερόβιον, καὶ Ἰνδῶν
τὸ ἁπλοῦν, ἀξιάγαστα.

Ζῆλος Ἡλιοῦ, Ἄβραμ τὸ φιλόθεον καὶ τὸ φιλόξενον, Ἰὼβ τὸ
μακρόθυμον, τοῦ Ἰωσὴφ δὲ τὸ φιλοπάρθενον, Μελχισεδὲκ τὸ ἅγιον, ἡ
ἡμερότης Μωσῆ, ἡ σοφία ἡ τοῦ Σολομῶντος δέ, κ' ἡ ἀνδρεία Σαμψών,
ἀξιάγαστα.

Ῥόδου Κολοσσός, τείχη Βαβυλώνια, ὁ κῆπος ὁ κρεμαστός, ὁ ναὸς
Ἀρτέμιδος, Μαυσώλου μνῆμα, Ζεὺς ἐλεφάντινος, ἡ πυραμίς,
λαβύρινθος, πύργος ὁ Φάρειος, Ἡρακλείας δὲ τὸ μονόλιθον, γῆς τὰ
θεάματα.

Λέοντος ἰσχύς, μελίσσης τὸ φίλεργον, ὁμοῦ καὶ μύρμηκος, ὄφεως τὸ
φρόνιμον, περιστερᾶς τε τὸ καθαρώτατον, τὸ τοῦ ἀρνίου ἄκακον, καὶ τὸ
κελάδημα ἀηδόνος, κ' ἡ πολλὴ ἡ ὅρασις ἀετοῦ, ἀληθῶς ἀξιάγαστα.

Χριστὲ Βασιλεῦ, ῥητῶν καὶ ἀρρήτων τε πραγμάτων παροχεῦ,
πλήθυνον, εὐλόγησον πόλεις καὶ νήσους καὶ τὰ γινόμενα, καὶ τοὺς
χρωμένους τούτοις δὲ ὅλους ἐλέησον, βροτούς, κτήνη, λογικὰ καὶ
ἄλογα, τῆς φιλτάτης Μητρός Σου δεήσεσι.

ODE IX "Every mortal born on earth"

Our faith and Turkish hospitality; French courts and Venetian aristocracy; Jewish solidarity, the Prussian army, and Scythian archery; English seamanship and the fairness of Spaniards are all so formidable.

Roman intellect, French artistry and ingenuity; Albanian prowess, Epirot prudence, Russian reverence, and the current war; Iberian liberty and Indian simplicity are all so formidable.

The zeal of Elijah, blessedness of Abraham, his kindness too; Job's forbearance and Joseph's protection of virgins; the sanctity of Melchizedek, meekness of Moses, wisdom of Solomon and Samson's valor and strength are all so formidable.

The Colossus of Rhodes, Babylon's walls and hanging gardens; the temple of Artemis, tomb of King Mausolus, and the ivory statue of Zeus; the pyramid, the labyrinth, the lighthouse of Alexandria and the monolithic theatre of Heraclea are the wonders of the world.

The lion's might, diligence of bee and ant alike; the vigilance of vipers, purity of doves and mildness of the lamb; the nightingale's song and the eagle's power of sight are truly formidable.

Christ our Lord, provider of things both spoken and unspoken, multiply and bless cities, islands, and goods. Have mercy on all who use them, be they reasoning mortals or speechless creatures, through the prayers of your beloved Mother.

ΕΞΑΠΟΣΤΕΙΛΑΡΙΟΝ «Τοῖς Μαθηταῖς»

Ὡς ἑκατὸν εὑρίσκονται, πόλεις, νῆσοι καὶ ὄρη, καὶ ἕως διακόσια
πράγματα καὶ πενήντα, ἐδῶ σ' αὐτὸν τὸν Κανόνα, κρασιά, ρακιά,
καρποὶ κι ἄλλα. Εὐφραίνεσθε καὶ χαίρεσθε, Ἀδελφοί, ταῦτα πάντα. Καὶ
τὰς καλὰς συμβουλίας ὅμως τὰς ἐν τῇ βίβλῳ ταύτῃ ἀναγινώσκετε, καὶ
ζῆτε ἐν Κυρίῳ.

Χριστιανῶν Βασίλισσα, καὶ ἀγάπη Μαρία, Σοὶ τὸ μικρὸν βιβλίον μου
ἀνατίθημι τοῦτο, τὰ λογικὰ ταῦτα δῶρα, Σὺ δὲ σκέπε καὶ σῷζε τοὺς
τοῦτο ἀντιγράφοντας ἀψευδῶς καὶ ἀσφάλτως, καὶ συνεχῶς, ἀγαπῶντας
τοῦτο ἀναγινώσκειν, εἰς ψυχικὴν ὠφέλειαν καὶ χαρὰν τῆς καρδίας.

Τέλος, τῷ δὲ Θεῷ ἀτελεύτητος δόξα.

ENVOY "To the disciples"

Near a hundred cities, islands, and mountains, near two hundred and fifty things are found in this canon of hymns: wines and spirits, fruits and more. Rejoice and delight, brothers, in all of these; and the fair counsels in this book may you heed, and live in the Lord.

Crown of Christians, beloved Mary, to You do I dedicate this little book of mine, these gifts of words. May You defend and deliver those who copy this work unfeignedly, unerringly, and those who will forever wish to read it for the benefit of their soul and rejoicing of their heart.

Glory be to God forever.

Εἴδησις*

Ἐπειδὴ πολλοὶ ἐπεχείρησαν πολλάκις πολλὰ βιβλία, παλαιά τε καὶ νέα, νὰ ἀντιγράψουσι, καὶ ἀντιγράφοντες αὐτὰ διαφθείρουσι, μὲ τὸ νὰ εἶναι ἀμαθεῖς, καὶ μὲ τὸ νὰ μὴ τὰ ξαναδιαβάζουσι μὲ τὸ πρωτότυπον, νὰ διορθώνουν τὰ λάθη, καὶ ἀντὶ καλὸν κάνουσι κακόν, καὶ ἀντὶς εὐχὴν λαμβάνουν ὀργήν. Καὶ ἐπειδὴ τινὲς πάλιν κλέπτουσι τὰ ξένα ποιήματα, τὰ οἰκειοποιοῦνται, καὶ τὰ ἐπιγράφουσι (φεῦ τῆς τόλμης) εἰς ὄνομά τους, καλλωπιζόμενοι, ὡς ὁ κολοιός, μὲ ξένα κάλλη οἱ ματαιόφρονες· καθὼς καὶ τοῦτο, μὲ λύπην τῆς καρδίας μου διὰ τὴν ἀσυνειδησίαν τους, ἔτυχε νὰ τὸ ἰδῶ εἰς μερικά μου ποιήματα. Καὶ ἐπειδὴ τὸ βιβλίον μου, Καθρέπτης γυνακῶν ὀνομαζόμενον, ὁποὺ τώρα νεωστί, εἰς τοὺς χιλίους ἑπτακοσίους ἑξηνταέξ, ἐτυπώθη εἰς Λιψίαν, ὁ ἀντιγραφεύς, ἢ ὁ τοῦ τύπου διορθωτής, ἐνόθευσεν αὐτὸ ὁ ἀσυνείδητος, τὸ διέφθειρε, τὸ ἀσχήμισε, τῆς πατρικῆς οὐσίας καὶ χάριτος τὸ ἐγύμνωσε, καὶ ἄλλο ἐξ ἄλλου τὸ ἔκαμεν, ἄλλα βάνοντας, ἄλλα εὐγάνοντας, καὶ ἄλλα ἀλλάζοντας, καθὼς ἡ δοκοφροσύνη, ἀνάθεμά την, τὸν ὑπαγόρευσε. Διὰ ταῦτα τὰ αἴτια ἀναγκάζομαι, Ἀδελφοί, εἰς τὸ τέλος τῶν βιβλίων μου, ὄντα ἕως τώρα ὑπὲρ τὰ δέκα, ... νὰ δίδω ταύτην τὴν εἴδησιν, καὶ νὰ γράφω τοῦτο τὸ ἐπιτίμιον, τὸ ὁποῖον παρακαλῶ πάντας, παρὰ πάντων να γράφεται. Ὅθεν καὶ εἰς τὸ τέλος τοῦ παρόντος γράφω καὶ λέγω, εἴ τις ἀγαπήσει, καὶ ἀντιγράψει καὶ τόδε πρὸς τοῖς ἄλλοις, καὶ δὲν τὸ ξαναδιαβάσει [μὲ] τὸ πρωτότυπον, νὰ μετρήσῃ τοὺς στίχους, καὶ νὰ διορθώσῃ τὰ λάθη, ὅτι ἀνάγκη, ὡς ἄνθρωπος, νὰ λανθάσῃ· ἢ ὅστις σφετερίσει, ἢ προσθέσει, ἢ ἀφαιρέσει, ἢ μετατρέψει, νὰ ἔχῃ ἀντίδικον τὸν Θεόν.

* The text of this passage is based on the first edition of Λόγοι πανηγυρικοί (1778), pp. 118–20.

Notice

There are many copyists who on many occasions have undertaken to copy books, both old and new ones, and in doing so have corrupted them, both out of ignorance and because they do not reread them against the original text in order to correct any mistakes. As a result, they do more harm than good and arouse anger instead of appreciation. Then again, there are certain people who also steal the compositions of others, appropriating them as their own and signing them with their own name (alas, what impudence). They are a vainglorious lot, who adorn themselves, as mackerel do, with the beauty of others. My heart aches with their shamelessness, as I have chanced to see this happen to some of my own compositions. As for my own book, *Mirror of Women*, which was only recently printed in Leipzig in 1766, an unscrupulous copyist or copy-editor corrupted, ruined and deformed my work, stripping it of its original essence and beauty. He turned it into something entirely different, adding and removing things here and there, and changing things round, driven as he was by vain conceit. For all these reasons, brothers, I am compelled to attach this notice at the end of my books, which now number more than ten, . . . and to write this reproof, asking everyone to copy it. This is why I am writing this at the end of the present book: whoever wishes to copy my work without checking it against the original, without counting the number of verses or correcting his mistakes (for to err is only human); or whoever appropriates, adds, removes, or changes anything, will be accountable before God.

ΕΠΙΣΤΟΛΑΙ ΔΙΑ ΣΤΙΧΩΝ ΑΠΛΩΝ ΚΑΤΑ ΤΗΣ ΥΠΕΡΗΦΑΝΕΙΑΣ ΚΑΙ ΠΕΡΙ ΜΑΤΑΙΟΤΗΤΟΣ ΚΟΣΜΟΥ/ LETTERS ON PRIDE AND THE VANITY OF HUMAN LIFE

Περὶ ματαιότητος κόσμου καὶ ἀθλιότητος τοῦ ἀνθρώπου*

Καπνὸς ὑπάρχει, Ἀδελφοί, ὁ βίος ὁποῦ ζοῦμεν.
Ὁ δρόμος εἶναι λιγοστὸς ὁποῦ περιπατοῦμεν.
Φθορά, σκιὰ τὰ πράγματα, αὐτὰ ὁποῦ κρατοῦμεν.
Ὄνειρο εἶναι, κορνιαρχτός, αὐτὰ ὁποῦ ζητοῦμεν.
Καὶ ταῖς χρυσαῖς ξοδιάζομεν ἡμέραις τῆς ζωῆς μας.
Καὶ χάνομεν ταῖς θεϊκαῖς χάριταις τῆς ψυχῆς μας.
Καὶ χαίρονται οἱ δαίμονες, οἱ Ἅγιοι λυποῦνται,
Οἱ Ἄγγελοι θαυμάζουσι, τὰ σύμπαντα κινοῦνται.
Δὲν εἶναι πρᾶγμα, Ἀδελφοί, τερπνὸν σ᾿ αὐτὸν τὸν βίον
Ὁποῦ νὰ μὴν ἐπέρασεν, ὡσὰν πουλί, ἢ πλοῖον,
Δὲν εἶναι εἰς τὴν γῆν ποτὲ γλυκάδα, εὐτυχία,
Ὁποῦ νὰ μὴν ἦναι μαζὶ καὶ λύπη καὶ πικρία.
Δὲν εἶναι δόξα, καὶ τιμή, ὁποῦ νὰ μὴ κρημνίσῃ,
Δὲν εἶναι κράτος δύναμις, ὁποῦ καὶ νὰ μὴ σβύσῃ.
Τί μάτην ταραττόμεθα λοιπόν, καὶ μεριμνοῦμεν;
Γιατί ἀγωνιζόμεθα ὡς τόσο, καὶ μοχθοῦμεν
Διὰ τὴν ματαιότητα τοῦ Κόσμου καὶ ἀπάτην,
Λύπην, καὶ πίκρα, καὶ φωτιὰ καὶ ἄνεμον γεμάτην.
Ὅταν τὸν Κόσμον, Ἀδελφοί, κερδήσωμεν τελείως,
Τότε τὸν τάφον μας γυμνοὶ οἰκήσομεν ἀθλίως.
Ὡσὰν ἄνθος μαραίνεται ἄνθρωπος ὁ καϊμένος,
Καὶ ὡσὰν ὄνειρο περνᾷ, πτωχός, κι εὐτυχισμένος.
Καὶ ἀναλεῖ σὰν τὸ κηρί, λυώνει σὰν τὸ χιόνι.
. . . .
Πάντα ἀπατηλότερα εἶναι τῶν ὀνειράτων.
Πάντα ὀγληγορώτερα σκιᾶς, καὶ τῶν ρευμάτων.
Μία στιγμή, καὶ ταῦτα δέ, πάντα τὰ εἰρημένα
Θάνατος τὰ κληρονομεῖ, καὶ δὲν μᾶς μένει ἕνα.
Δὲν συνοδεύει ἡ δόξα μας, εἰμὴ ὡς τὸ μνημεῖον.

* The extracts are based on Frantzi 1993; they correspond to lines 9–31, 41–49, 61–72, 75–86, 119–30, 133–44, 163–84, 391–412, and 495–506 of Dapontes's text.

On the Vanity of the World and the Woes of Man

Our life, o brethren, is a wisp of smoke,
And the path we tread is all too short.
Shadows and rot are the things we possess,
Dreams full of dust are the things that we seek.
We fritter away the golden days of our life
And fail to attain the godly grace of our soul.
The demons rejoice while the saints lament,
And angels admire as the universe moves.
My brethren, no delight in life is there
That does not glide away like bird or boat.
There is no sweet or happy thing on earth
That is not mixed with bitterness or woe.
No honor or fame that has not led to ruin,
Nor rule or sway that has not faded away.
So why in vain be troubled? Why be anxious?
Yet, all the same, we struggle, strive and toil
For vanity and for the world's deception,
For grief and gloom, all filled with wind and fire.
When we will overcome this world for good,
Naked and wretched will we dwell in our tomb.
For like a flower that wilts is hapless man,
And, poor or blest, he passes like a dream.
He burns like a candle and melts like snow.
. . . .
All is more illusive than the stuff of dreams,
All more fleeting than shadows or streams.
In an instance, all that has been said
Death acquires, and we are left with naught.
Our fame does not escort us to the grave.

Δὲν ἔρχεται ὁ πλοῦτος μας στοῦ ἄδου τὸ ταμεῖον.
Μάταια τὰ ἀνθρώπινα πάντα καὶ ματαιότης,
Τέλος κι αὐτὸς ὁ ἄνθρωπος μάταιος, ἀθλιότης.
Τί μάτην ταραττόμεθα λοιπόν, καὶ μεριμνοῦμεν;
....
Ὅταν τὸν Κόσμον, Ἀδελφοί, κερδήσωμεν τελείως,
Τότε τὸν τάφον μας γυμνοὶ οἰκήσομεν ἀθλίως.
Γυμνοὶ ὅλοι ἐβγήκαμεν μὲ τὸ κορμί μας μόνον,
Ἀπ᾽ τὴν κοιλιὰ τῆς μάνας μας, ἀπ᾽ τοῦ Ἀδὰμ τὸν χρόνον.
Γυμνοὶ πάλιν ἐμπαίνομεν στὴν γῆν ἀποθαμένοι.
Γῆ εἴμεσθεν, καὶ εἰς τὴν γῆν καθ᾽ εἷς πάλιν πηγαίνει,
Καὶ βασιλεύς, καὶ ἡγεμών, καὶ πλούσιος, καὶ πένης,
Πάντες οἱ ἄνθρωποι τῆς γῆς, πάσης τῆς οἰκουμένης.
Τί μάτην ταραττόμεθα λοιπὸν καὶ μεριμνοῦμεν;
Γιατί ἀγωνιζόμεθα ὡς τόσο, καὶ μοχθοῦμεν
Διὰ τὴν ματαιότητα τοῦ Κόσμου και ἀπάτην,
Λύπη, καὶ πίκρα, καὶ φωτιά, καὶ ἄνεμον γεμάτην;
....
Ὕπαγε εἰς τὰ μνήματα, σῦρε εἰς τὰ ταφεῖα,
Καὶ ἴδε τίς ὁ βασιλεύς, καὶ τί ἡ βασιλεία.
Ὁ θρόνος ποῦ; τὸ σκῆπτρον ποῦ; χλαμὺς ποῦ, καὶ πορφύρα;
Ποῦ στέμμα, καὶ διάδημα; ποῦ δὲ καὶ ἡ πλημμύρα;
Χρυσοῦ, ἀργύρου, καὶ λοιπῶν, πολυτελῶν πραγμάτων,
Παρεστηκότων, φαγητῶν, στρωμάτων, φορεμάτων.
Ποῦ τὸ σπαθί, ποῦ προσταγή; καὶ ποῦ τὸ ἔτζι θέλω.
Ἔτζι ὁρίζω καὶ γενῇ, ὁ βασιλεὺς γὰρ πέλω.
Λαοῦ ποῦ ἡ προσκύνησις; Ἀρχόντων ποῦ δειλία;
Ποῦ Πρέσβεις; ποῦ οἱ ἔπαινοι; καὶ ποῦ ἡ κολακεία;
Ποῦ οἱ σωματοφύλακες; ποῦ ἡ μεγαλειότης;
Ποῦ κρότοι; ποῦ τὰ θέατρα, καὶ ἡ λοιπὴ λαμπρότης;
....
Θυμήσου τὸν Ἀλέξανδρον, τὸν μέγαν Μακεδόνα.
Ἐτοῦτος βασιλέα μου ἐκεῖνον τὸν αἰῶνα,
Τὸν Διογένην εὕρηκεν, ὁποῦ περιπατοῦσε

Our riches follow not to Hades's house.
Vain are all things human, all is vanity;
Man himself is vain, and all is misery.
So why in vain be troubled? Why be anxious?
. . . .
When we will overcome this world for good
Naked and wretched we will dwell in our tomb.
Naked we all emerged from our mother's womb,
With only our body, since Adam's time.
Naked again we return to earth at death.
For earth we are and to earth each returns,
The king and the prince, the rich and the poor,
Everyone on earth, in the entire world.
So why in vain be troubled? Why be anxious?
Yet, all the same, we struggle, strive and toil
For vanity and for the world's deception,
For grief and gloom, all filled with wind and fire.
. . . .
Go to the tombs and walk around the graves,
Look for the king and all his kingdom.
Where are the throne, the sceptre, cloak and robes?
Where is the crown and diadem? The heap
Of gold and silver and other precious things?
Where are the food, feasts, raiments and attendants?
Where is sword and mandate? Where the sudden whim:
"My wish is my command, for I am king"?
Where is the subjects' worship, and dread of timid lords?
Where are the ministers, the flattery and praise?
Where are the guards? His Majesty himself?
The cheers and spectacles and splendour everywhere?
. . . .
Remember Alexander the Great.
This Macedonian, centuries past,
Chanced upon Diogenes wandering about

Τοὺς τάφους τοὺς βασιλικούς, κι ἕνα ῥαβδὶ βαστοῦσε.
Κι ἐσκάλιζε μὲ τὸ ῥαβδὶ ἐκεῖ εἰς τὰ μνημεῖα,
Τάχα πῶς κάτι τι ζητεῖ, καὶ ἐν ἐπιμελείᾳ.
Τὸν ἐρωτᾷ ὁ βασιλεύς, λέγωντας, τί γυρεύει;
Τὸν ἀποκρίνεται αὐτὸς δίχως νὰ κολακεύῃ,
Τὴν κεφαλήν, Ἀλέξανδρε, Φιλίππου τοῦ πατρός σου
Ζητῶ μὲ ἐπιμέλειαν, ὡς βλέπεις καὶ ἀτός σου.
Καὶ ἀπ' ταῖς ἄλλαις δὲν 'μπορῶ νὰ τὴν ἐξεχωρίσω,
Ὅλαις γυμναῖς, ὀστᾶ ξηρά, πόθεν καὶ τὴν γνωρίσω;
. . . .
Πήγαινε εἰς τὰ μνήματα, σῦρε εἰς τὰ ταφεῖα,
Καὶ ἴδε τίς ὁ ἡγεμὼν καὶ τί ἡγεμονεία.
Ποῦ τὸ σκαμνί; ποῦ ἡ τιμή; καὶ ποῦ ἡ ἐξουσία;
Ποῦ Μολδοβία ἡ λαμπρά, ποῦ ἡ κλεινὴ Βλαχία,
Ποῦ τὸ τοπούζι; ποῦ σπαθί; ποῦ ἡ δορυφορία;
Ποῦ τὰ φιλοδωρήματα, καὶ ἡ δωροφορία;
Ποῦ Ἄρχοντες; ποῦ Στρατηγοί; καὶ ποῦ οἱ στρατιῶτες;
Ποῦ οἱ σωροὶ τῶν φαγητῶν; ποῦ οἱ περιεστῶτες;
Ποῦ τὰ χρυσοχαλίνωτα ἄλογα, καὶ θρεμμένα,
Ἀπὸ τὸν ἄνθρωπον πολλὰ πλιὸ ἐπιμελημένα;
Ποῦ τὰ χρυσᾶ ἁμάξια τὰ πορφυρονտυμένα;
Ἀπ' τῶν πτωχῶν τὰ σπήτια πολλὰ πλιὸ στολισμένα;
. . . .
Εἰπέ μας, τίνος τὰ γυμνά, καὶ καταξηραμένα
Εἶναι ἐτοῦτα κόκκαλα, καὶ καταφρονεμένα;
Τοῦτο εἶναι ἡ περίφημος ἐκείνη ἡ Ἑλένη.
Δι' ἣν τοσοῦτοι πόλεμοι, καὶ φόνοι εἶχαν γένει.
Καὶ ἡ πανωλεθρία δὲ ἐκείνης τῆς Τρωάδος.
Αὐτ' εἶναι ἡ Ἑλένη, ναί, τὸ θαῦμα τῆς Ἑλλάδος.
Αὐτ' εἶναι ἡ ἄβυσσος ἐκείνων τῶν χαρίτων.
Αὐτ' εἶναι ὁ παράδεισος τόσων ὡραιοτήτων.
Τοῦτ' ἡ ξηρὰ ἡ κάρα; ναί; ἐτοῦτο τὸ κρανίον,
Δίχως μορφήν, κάλλους χωρίς, θήκη τῶν σκουληκίων.
Μὰ πῶς ἔτζι ἐσβύσθηκαν τὰ ὄμματα Ἑλένης,

The royal tombs with walking stick in hand.
He saw him poking in the tombs with this,
As if in search of something earnestly.
The king then asked him what it was he sought,
And he replied, with no attempt to fawn,
"It is your father Philip's skull I seek
With such intent, as you can see yourself.
But I cannot distinguish it from all the rest.
How could I? All are bare and dried-up bones."
. . . .
Go to the tombs and walk around the graves,
Look for the prince and his principality.
Where is his chair of state, his honor and command?
The fine and famed Moldavia and Wallachia?
Where are the staff and sword and retinue?
The bestowal of gifts and offerings?
The generals, the soldiers and the lords?
Where are the attendants and the heaps of food?
Where are the horses, gold-harnessed and fine-bred,
Taken care of more than man himself?
Where are the gold and purple-covered carriages,
Decked out more than the houses of the poor?
. . . .
Do tell us, whose are these deserted,
Shrivelled up, and much-detested bones?
To far-renowned Helen they belong,
For whom so many wars and deaths occurred
As well as the entire ruin of Troy.
Yes, this is Helen, the beauty of Greece.
This is the pit where all her grace now lies,
This is the paradise of so much charm.
This parched-up pate? Indeed. This skull is hers
Devoid of form or grace; a case for worms.
How could the eyes of Helen vanish thus,

Ὁποῦ, ὡς ἄστρα, ἄστραπταν ὅλης τῆς οἰκουμένης;
Πῶς χάθηκε τὸ πρόσωπον, ὁποῦ τῆς εὐμορφίας
Ἐστάθη τὸ πρωτότυπον χωρίς ἀντιλογίας;
Πῶς ἔτζι ἐμαράνθηκαν τὰ ρόδα ὀπ' ἀνθοῦσαν
Στὰ δύο της τὰ μάγουλα, κι ἐροδοκοκκινοῦσαν,
Ποῦ εἶναι τόσαις χάριτες, ὁποῦ στὸ μέτωπόν της
Ἐχόρευαν, μὲ ἔρωτα ὅλων τῶν θεωρῶν της;
Ποῦ ἡ πορφύρα ἡ πολλή, ὁποῦ τὰ δυό της χείλη
Ἐστόλιζε, κι ἔτριζαν τὰ δόντια τους οἱ φίλοι;
Ποῦ εἶν' ἐκείνη ἡ ξανθὴ κόμη, ὁποῦ, ὡς ἕνα
Χρυσοπλεμένο δίκτυον, ψάρευε τὸν καθένα;
....
Γεννᾶται μὲ τὰ δάκρυα, δακρύωντας πεθαίνει,
Μὲ πάθη ἀναθρέφεται, μὲ πειρασμοὺς αὐξαίνει.
Τὴν γέννησίν του ἀγνοεῖ, τὸ εἶναι του δὲν ἠξεύρει,
Τὸν θάνατόν του δὲν νοεῖ, πότε θέλει τὸν εὕρει.
Ἡμέραις του ὡσὰν σκιά, ὁ βίος σὰν ποτάμι,
Σείεται καὶ κλονίζεται πάντοτε σὰν καλάμι.
Ὡσὰν τὸ ἄνθος τοῦ ἀγροῦ φυτρώνει καὶ αὐξάνει,
Ὡς ἄνθος καὶ μαραίνεται, πολὺν καιρὸν δὲν κάνει.
Εὐθὺς ἀνθεῖ καὶ ἀπανθεῖ, ξηραίνετ' αἰφνιδίως,
Ὡς ἡ σελήνη φθίνει δέ, ὡς ὄνειρον ὁ βίος.
Βίος σκιώδης καὶ ψευδής, ζωὴ πολλὰ ἀθλία,
Ζωὴ παγίδων καὶ πολλῶν γεμάτη, καὶ ἀχρεία.
Νῦν χαίρω, πάντα δὲ πονῶ, γελῶ, καὶ παίζω τώρα,
Πικραίνομαι, καὶ κλαίω δὲ εἰσὲ ὀλίγην ὥρα.
Ἀκμάζω νῦν, ἀσθενῶ δὲ παντοτινὰ ἀθλίως.
Νῦν τώρα ζῶ, πεθαίνω δὲ ἔξαφνα αἰφνιδίως.
Νῦν τώρα φαίνομαι καλά, φαίνομ' εὐτυχισμένος,
Πάντα δὲ κακοροίζικος, καὶ κακομοιριασμένος.
Ὡς τόσο μεταβάλλονται τὰ πάντα καὶ γυρίζουν.
Ὡς τόσην τὰ ἀνθρώπινα μεταβολὴν γνωρίζουν.
Ὁπ' οὐδὲ μίαν ὥραν κἂν δὲν στέκονται, δὲν μένουν
Εἰς τὴν αὐτὴν κατάστασιν, εὐθὺς τροπὴν λαβαίνουν.

Which shone like stars throughout the world entire?
How could her face be lost, whose loveliness
Became a paragon, beyond all doubt?
How could the roses that did bloom and blush
On both her cheeks thus wilt and waste away?
Where is the beauty that on her brow
Once used to sparkle, charming her admirers?
Where is the crimson glow that used to beam
On her two lips, while friends would gnash their teeth?
Where are those golden locks that like a
Gilded fishing net would lure and catch each man?
. . . .
Man cries at birth and cries again at death,
With passions and temptations he is reared.
His birth and being he does not understand
And has no thought of when his death will come.
His days are shadows, his life a river,
He always sways and trembles like a reed.
Like a flower in a field he sprouts and grows,
Like a flower he withers away; his time is brief.
He blooms, then fades and quickly shrivels up.
Like the moon he wanes; his life is like a dream;
Shadowy, illusory, and full of woes,
His life is wretched, filled with wiles and snares.
Now I rejoice, laugh and play but suffer still,
For shortly I repine and start to weep.
I thrive for now yet weaken all the time.
Now I am alive but death is sudden and abrupt.
I seem at present cheerful and content,
But ever hapless and ill-starred I go.
All things change and turn around.
So many changes come to human life
That even for an hour things do not stay
The same but take an unexpected turn.

....
Ὅ,τι καλὸν καὶ ἄν κρατῇς τῆς γῆς, αὐτοῦ τοῦ κόσμου,
Οὐδὲν κρατεῖς, ναὶ Ἀδελφέ, ναί, μάρτυς ὁ Θεός μου.
Ὅτι καθὼς ἡ θάλασσα δὲν στέκ᾽ εἰς μίαν στάσιν,
Ἔτζι καὶ τὰ ἐγκόσμια, δὲν ἔχουν ποτὲ βάσιν.
Καθὼς ἡ φούσκαις τοῦ νεροῦ σκάζουσι δὲν βαστοῦσι,
Ἔτζι καὶ τὰ ἐγκόσμια, ἡ πέτραις τὸ βοοῦσι.
Καθὼς τὸ χιώνι τὴν δροσιὰν ὁ Ἥλιος τὴν λυώνει,
Ἔτζι καὶ τὰ ἐγκόσμια, καὶ ποῖος δὲν τὸ νοιώνει.
Καθὼς τὰ ἴχνη τοῦ πουλιοῦ δὲν βρίσκονται, καὶ πλοίου,
Ἔτζι καὶ τὰ ἐγκόσμια, καὶ ὅλα τὰ τοῦ βίου.
Καθὼς τὸ ὄνειρο πετᾷ εὐθὺς ὁπού ξυπνοῦμεν,
Ἔτζι καὶ τὰ ἐγκόσμια αὐτὰ νὰ τὰ θαρροῦμεν.

. . . .
Whatever goodness in this world you hold,
Naught it is indeed; witness is my God.
The sea is never still and like the sea
Are worldly things as well; they have no base.
As water bubbles burst and do not last,
So worldly things do too; the stones cry it out.
As the frosty snow melts under the sun,
So worldly things do too; everyone knows.
Like the lost traces of a bird or boat
Are earthly things and all the cares of life.
As a dream that flees as soon as we awake
Should we consider worldly matters too.

Notes

≈

Extract from "Geographical History"

Bab-i-Humayun   Turkish name for the Sublime Gate, main entrance to the Seraglio, which was the residence of the Sultan in Constantinople and was also used to host important state events, such as the one described here. The first court of the palace contained various functional buildings, including a hospital, bakery, arsenal (mentioned in lines 3–4), and the Imperial Mint   (*darphane* in Turkish; hence "ταραπχανᾶ," in line 5). This building was erected in 1727, a modern construction at the time of Dapontes's visit.

Prince Ioannes   Younger brother of Konstantinos Mavrokordatos, in whose court in Jassy and Bucharest Dapontes had served as *grammatikos* from 1731 to 1743.

vizier   Presumably the Grand Vizier. He was the Sultan's chief minister in the Ottoman government and head of the divan, the Imperial Council. The ulema, the scholars trained in Islamic sacred law and theology, were one of the three groups of the Ottoman ruling class represented in the divan. The significance of Tuesday is unclear (presumably one of the designated days on which the Imperial Council met). Unclear too is the precise meaning of "καλαμπά"— possibly related to "καλαμπαλίκι," from the Turkish *kalabalık* (crowd), hence the translation "thronged." The "square" in the following line is a translation of the Greek "μεϊντάνι," from the Turkish *meydan*.

High up ... nor appearing   Following the principle of imperial seclusion, the Sultan never attended the council meetings himself but listened to the proceedings from behind a grilled window covered by a red curtain.

janissaries   The Sultan's elite infantry— in effect, his household troops and bodyguards. Although originally consisting of prisoners of war, janissaries came to enjoy many privileges and were paid handsomely for their military services. The handing out of their pay (*ulûfe* in Turkish, hence "λουφὲς") took place every three months and was itself a special ceremony which involved a special meal with soup (*çorba* in Turkish, hence "τζορβᾶς"), a dish that carried a symbolic significance among the janissaries. The reception of ambassadors (*elçi* in Turkish, hence "ἐλτζήδαις") or other foreign officials was usually arranged for the same day, as it was an opportunity for the Sultan to display the state's wealth. It is no coincidence then that the inauguration of Prince Ioannes took place on the janissaries' payday.

imperial caftan and the crest   The high point of the ceremony was when the Sultan vested the prince with a type of caftan and a jeweled, feathered crest (*kuka* in Turkish), both highly symbolic of the new prince's new status.

club   An ornate club (*topuz* in Turkish) used by Ottomans on horseback. Like Dapontes, contemporary travelers to Constantinople were impressed by the ornamentation of imperial horses. The following description by the French traveler Aubry de La Motraye (1674–1747) helps us imagine what Dapontes himself would have seen:

> [The horses] ... were generally very richly equipped, and their Bridles, Saddles, etc. not only glitter'd with Gems, but they had ... on the right Side of the Saddle, in the Place where we put our Pistols, a Topouz of Silver gilt ... embellish'd with Rubies, and other precious

> Stones upon a Sabre which lay along the Horses flank.
> ... The Stirrups were generally Silver gilt, as well as all
> other Parts of the Trappings, and enriched with Gems;
> in short, 'twas one of the most magnificent and glori-
> ous Sights that (I believe) can be had. (*Travels through
> Europe, Asia, and into Part of Africa ...*, London 1723:
> 1.183)

Phanari   The quarter in Constantinople, near the Patriarchate,
where the elite Greek families resided and from which their collec-
tive name derives. For a colourful, though disparaging description
of the prince's majestic arrival in his newly-appointed province,
consistent with the pomp surrounding the inauguration ceremony in
Constantinople, see Zallony 1826: 291–93.

royal military band   Dapontes's "μεχτερχανὲ" is from the Turkish
mehterhane (marching band).

Mirror of Women

Susanna

Susanna   Dapontes's narrative is based on the Apocryphal story
of Susanna, an addition (chapter 13) to the Greek version of the
Book of Daniel. Most stories in the *Mirror of Women* are based on
Apocryphal literature.

Like two black crows around a snowy dove   One cannot help recalling
Shakespeare's Romeo here comparing Juliet's exquisite beauty to "a
snowy dove trooping with crows" (1.5.47).

Koukouzelis   St. Ioannes Koukouzelis (ca. 1280–1360), chanter and
composer, known for his influential reforms of Orthodox Church
music and his enchanting voice.

Bathsheba   Wife of Uriah and later of King David. Like Susanna,
Bathsheba attracted the attention of an onlooker (David) while

bathing outdoors, which is why Chariton is reminded of her at this point in the story. To emphasize Susanna's virtue, Dapontes reminds his readers of the two women's different reactions: unlike Susanna, Bathsheba submitted to David's seductive advances (2 Sam. 11:1–5).

villains   A rendering of the unknown word "ταϊφάλοι," most likely from Turkish and possibly related to *tayf* (phantom).

child   Daniel, prophet and protagonist in the Book of Daniel. Dapontes does not mention his name until line 881, and he describes him repeatedly as a "small child" (rather than the young man he is in the original story), possibly to enhance the dramatic effect.

The child called Samuel   A reference to the story of Samuel, servant of the priest Eli who had two wayward sons. God had chosen Samuel to take Eli's place when the latter's house would be destroyed as a result of his sons' transgressions and he called Samuel one night to reveal his plan (1 Sam. 3).

mastic tree . . . you be cut in two   Dapontes reproduces the pun made in the original Greek text between the words "σχοῖνον" (mastic tree) and "σχίση" (cut in two). He creates the same ironic effect below, in the interrogation with the second elder, with the pun on the words "πρῖνον" (oak tree) and "πριονίση" (saw you down).

Garden of Graces

BOOK FIVE

On My Withdrawal from the World

King of Rome   Numa Pompilius, the legendary king of Rome. From Plutarch's description one can see why Dapontes would have felt an affinity with this ruler:

> By natural temperament he was inclined to the practice
> of every virtue, and he had subdued himself still more
> by discipline, endurance of hardships, and the study of

wisdom. . . . He banished from his house all luxury and extravagance, and . . . he devoted his hours of privacy and leisure, not to enjoyments and money-making, but to the service of the gods, and the rational contemplation of their nature and power. . . .

. . . Forsaking the ways of city folk, [Numa] determined to live for the most part in country places, and to wander there alone, passing his days in groves of the gods, sacred meadows, and solitudes. ("Numa," in *Lives*, trans. Bernadotte Perrin, vol. 1, Loeb Classical Library, Cambridge, MA: Harvard University Press, 1914: 3.5–4.1)

farms   The Greek word "τζιφτιλίκι" comes from the Turkish *çiflik* (farm).

Artaxerxes   Artaxerxes Mnemon (404–358 BC), king of Persia. On the incident referred to by Dapontes, see Plutarch, "Sayings of Kings and Commanders: Artaxerxes Mnemon," in Moralia, 3:174A.

BOOK ELEVEN

In Praise of Samos

Samos   Dapontes arrived on Samos on December 4, 1764, during his alms-collecting mission and stayed on the island for five months.

Alexandros   The *Garden of Graces* was dedicated to Alexandros, fourteen-year-old son of Ioannes Mavrokordatos, in whose court in Moldavia Dapontes had served in 1743. This explains why Dapontes also addresses him as a "young bey".

temple   The temple of Hera on Samos, built in the sixth century BC.

column in Byzantium   The column of Constantine, erected in the forum in the center of the city.

famous monolithic column   The Egyptian obelisk re-erected by Theodosius I in the hippodrome of Constantinople in the fourth century AD. The four bronze legs are a reference to the blocks of bronze that were placed on each corner of the obelisk's base.

Egypt's pyramids . . . in stately style   When Egypt became a Roman province in 30 BC, a number of obelisks were removed and taken to Rome to embellish the city and assert imperial authority.

Valide Han   The Buyuk Valide Han, one of Constantinople's largest caravansarays built near the Grand Bazaar in the seventeenth century.

cave in the Peloponnese   Probably a reference to the famous "Cave of the Lakes" near Kalavryta in the northern Peloponnese.

Andros   "ἄντρον," the ancient word for "cave."

the five-year silence   Pythagorean teaching emphasized the importance of silence as a means of attaining self-control. According to later tradition, those who wanted to be initiated in the Pythagorean brotherhood had to observe a five-year silence.

Panegyrics

Canon of Hymns Containing Many Exceptional Things

ODE I

wine of the isle of Skopelos   Attached as he was to his homeland, Dapontes gives the island's wine pride of place (cf. *Garden of Graces*, 11.17, 14.27).

commandaria from Cyprus   Dapontes would probably have tasted this rich dessert wine at princely banquets in Moldavia and Wallachia; it was made from indigenous varieties of grapes grown in Cyprus. He was always one to "enjoy good food and good wine" (*Garden of Graces*, 9.197–98).

Samian muscat   Dapontes was not the only one to praise this sweet and musky white wine, which he enjoyed during his extended stay on Samos in 1764 (*Garden of Graces*, 11.13–18); cf. Lord Byron's "Fill high the cup with Samian wine!" ("The Isles of Greece," in *Don Juan*, 3.86.9).

vodka of Danzig   Later known as Gdańsk, this coastal city in northern Poland was home to "Danziger Goldwasser," a root and herbal spirit first produced in the late sixteenth century. Famous for its flakes of gold, the beverage was popular in the royal courts of Europe. In the eighteenth century, large quantities were exported to Moldavia, which is where Dapontes would probably have tasted it himself.

rosolios of Corfu   A rich cordial made from cinnamon, raisins, rose petals, and cloves, rosolio was produced in Corfu under the Venetians. It is also cited as a luxury product in other contemporary literary works; see, for example, Carlo Goldoni, *La Villeggiatura* (1761), III.17.

mastic   Dapontes visited Chios and its mastic-producing villages in July 1764 during his alms-collecting mission (*Garden of Graces*, 10.27–28, 43–46). Chios was the wealthiest island in the Aegean due to its monopoly of the mastic trade and its special tax privileges granted by the Sublime Porte. See Dimitrios G. Ierapetritis, "The Geography of the Chios Mastic Trade from the 17th through to the 19th Century," *Ethnobotany Research and Applications* 8 (2010): 153–67.

Smyrna sultanas   One of the most commercially vibrant cities in the Ottoman Empire, Smyrna was one of the largest producers of figs and raisins. The pale yellow, seedless variety had acquired an international reputation from the late sixteenth century when it started being exported by English merchants of the Levant Company, which had secured the exclusive right to trade in Smyrna sultanas. In modern poetry, the dried fruit found a place in the pocket of the unshaven Smyrna merchant, Mr. Eugenides (T. S. Eliot, *The Waste Land*, 3.209–11).

pears of Mount Sinai   The fertile land at the foot of Mount Sinai produced large quantities of fruit, including pears "of excellent quality," as noted by Carsten Niebuhr, a contemporary German traveler (*Travels through Arabia, and Other Countries in the East*, ..., trans. Robert Heron, Edinburgh 1792: 1.190). Dapontes himself never traveled as far as Egypt, but Mount Sinai was such a popular destination that pilgrims and travelers would have quickly spread information about the land.

melons of Vodena   Vodena, historical name for the city of Edessa in northern Greece, was linked to a melon variety known as *vodina cavun*, large and long in shape, which was cultivated in Constantinople. Not to be confused with Edessa, ancient city in Mesopotamia, whose melons also happened to be renowned for their size; the seventh-century archbishop Theodore of Tarsus had remarked that "they grow so large that a camel can scarcely carry two of them" (quoted in *Biblical Commentaries from the Canterbury School of Theodore and Hadrian*, ed. by Bernhard Bischoff and Michael Lapidge, Cambridge: Cambridge University Press, 1994: 35).

Bursa's chestnuts   First capital of the Ottoman Empire, located near the southern coast of the Sea of Marmara, Bursa was a commercially vibrant city noted also for its large number of chestnut trees, frequently mentioned by contemporary travelers. See Heath W. Lowry, *Ottoman Bursa in Travel Accounts*, Bloomington: Indiana University Ottoman and Modern Turkish Studies Publications, 2003: 51–56.

Aleppo's pistachios   Contemporary travelers often remarked on the superior quality of the pistachios produced in large quantities in the Syrian city of Aleppo. See, for instance, [Alessandro Bisani], *A Picturesque Tour through Part of Europe, Asia, and Africa...*, London: R. Faulder, 1793: 109.

Kios's pomegranates   Site of ancient Cius (now known as Gemlik), a town north of Bursa. Its pomegranates were held in such high esteem that, according to a contemporary source, the inhabitants of the area were "obliged to pay their personal impost with a certain quantity of this fruit, which they send every year to Constantinople, for the harem of the Grand Seignior" (Henry A. S. Dearborn, *A Memoir on the Commerce and Navigation of the Black Sea, and the Trade and Maritime Geography of Turkey and Egypt*, Boston: Wells and Lilly, 1819: 2:29).

apricots and damsons of Damascus   One of the major meeting points on the pilgrimage route to Mecca, Damascus was praised by local writers in the eighteenth century for its abundant supply of fresh fruit, which included the famous damson plum, cultivated there since antiquity. See James Grehan, *Everyday Life and Consumer Culture in Eighteenth-Century Damascus*, Seattle: University of Washington Press, 2007: 109–10.

ODE III

Snake stones and porcupine bezoars   A reference to the bones from the head of the cobra, believed in eastern folklore to act as antidotes against poisonous snake bites. Bezoars, small stony concretions formed inside the stomach of certain animals, were also believed to act as antidotes. They were in high demand in the seventeenth century and valued as exotic commodities. The bezoar of the porcupine from the Indian province of Malacca was particularly prized; even fakes were sold at inordinate prices.

Mecca's balsam   Spice obtained from the gum of the Commiphora tree in southern Arabia; celebrated since antiquity for its aromatic and medicinal properties.

China's musk   An exclusive ingredient in the preparation of perfume and one of the most precious goods imported into the Ottoman Empire, its sensuous properties have often been celebrated in

Ottoman lyric poetry. See Walter G. Andrews, Najaat Black, and Mehmet Kalpakli, eds. and trans., *Ottoman Lyric Poetry: An Anthology*, expanded ed., Seattle: University of Washington Press, 2006: 39, 135, 167.

Venetian treacle   An expensive concoction supposedly based on an ancient formula, its name derives from the Greek word "θηριακή" (theriaca), denoting an antidote against poisonous bites. Consisting of more than seventy herbs, roots, flowers, spices, and some rather unusual ingredients (such as dried vipers), all mixed in honey, the preparation was hailed as a panacea for a range of ailments, and was in high demand in the Ottoman Empire. On Ottoman documents advertising its miraculous properties, see Edhem Eldem, *French Trade in Istanbul in the Eighteenth Century*, Leiden: Brill, 1999: 86nn71–72.

England's typography   In western Europe of the eighteenth century, England had become the center of typographic activity, especially after the innovations of the English typographers William Caslon (1692–1766) and John Baskerville (1706–1775). Dapontes's appreciation of the art of printing is certainly linked to the great pride that he took in the publication of his own books. It may also stem from his first-hand acquaintance with Greek printing presses: a small press was set up in the Phanar quarter of Constantinople in 1763, coinciding with his extended stay in the capital. Although short-lived, set up as it was for polemical purposes in the context of a brief religious controversy, this printing press may well have had links with an earlier one that was established in Constantinople in the seventeenth century by Patriarch Cyril Lucaris and the cleric Nikodemos Metaxas. That press was actually shipped from London by Metaxas, who had already printed Greek books in England with prominent printers of his day. See Evro Layton, "Nikodemos Metaxas, the First Greek Printer in the Eastern World," *Harvard Library Bulletin* 15 (1967): 140–68.

quinces of Adrianople   When Dapontes stayed in Adrianople (modern-day Edirne) in 1757, at the start of his mission, he would have had the opportunity to taste quince preserve, a delicacy often commented on by travelers: "The manufacturers of Adrianople are chiefly engrossed by the preparation of . . . costly comfits, made of quinces, which are sent all over Turkey as a celebrated sweetmeat" ([Friedrich] von Tietz, *St. Petersburgh, Constantinople, and Napoli di Romania in 1833 and 1834 . . .*, trans. J. D. Haas, New York: Theodore Foster, 1836: 103).

olives of Crete   Crete was the empire's largest producer of olives and olive oil, with exports increasing dramatically in the first two decades of the eighteenth century, partly in response to the growing soap industry in France. See Tülay Artan, "Aspects of the Ottoman Elite's Food Consumption: Looking for 'Staples,' 'Luxuries,' and 'Delicacies' in a Changing Century," in *Consumption Studies and the History of the Ottoman Empire, 1550–1922: An Introduction*, ed. Donald Quataert, Albany: State University of New York Press, 2000: 145–49.

oxen of Moldavia   Moldavia was one of the centers of the cattle trade in the seventeenth and eighteenth centuries, with large herds being exported as far as Frankfurt and Poland. See Bruce McGowan, "Ottoman Exports to Pre-Industrial Europe," in *Economic Life in Ottoman Europe: Taxation, Trade and the Struggle for Land, 1600–1800*, Cambridge: Cambridge University Press, 1981: 26. Dapontes may also have had in mind the aurochs, a type of wild ox, which became the traditional symbol of Moldavia, appearing on coats of arms and on the frontispieces of books printed in the principalities. The figure of an aurochs's head appears in Dapontes's Βιβλίον περιέχον τὰς ἱερὰς ἀκολουθίας . . . (Bucharest, 1736).

kashkaval   A type of hard, yellow, full-fat traditional cheese made from sheep's milk.

caviar of Vidin   A town on the southern bank of the Danube on the northwest tip of Bulgaria, Vidin was one of the main producers of caviar; it would have supplied the nearby cities of Bucharest and Veliko Trnovo where Dapontes had stayed. Commenting on the impressive size of the fish, a later British traveler wrote:

> A staple article of export from Widdin [Vidin] is cavi-are, which is obtained in enormous quantities from the roe of the sturgeon, and sent away packed in barrels on board the flat-bottomed boats that ply up the river. I have seen a sturgeon fully twelve feet long caught in the Danube. Three men were dragging it with a rope through the streets of Widdin. (Charles S. Ryan, *Under the Red Crescent: Adventures of an English Surgeon with the Turkish Army at Plevna and Erzeroum, 1877–1878*, London: John Murray, 1897: 59)

On the popularity of caviar among contemporary Greeks, the French traveler François Pouqueville wrote: "As to the caviar, it may be considered as the national dish; and he would be badly treated, who should speak of it with disrespect" (*Travels through the Morea, Albania, and Several Other Parts of the Ottoman Empire . . .*, translator unknown, London: Richard Phillips, 1806: 71).

fish of Aenus The coastal town of Aenus (modern-day Enez) on the southeastern coast of Thrace was Dapontes's first stop after setting sail from Mount Athos in May 1757. During his three-day stay, he "wined and dined with the bishop and praised the abundance of fish in the area" (*Garden of Graces*, 6.27–28).

Aretsou Modern-day Derince, a port town in the easternmost extremity of the Sea of Marmara, near the ancient city of Nicomedia.

sturgeons of Azov The Sea of Azov, north of the Black Sea, was renowned for its large quantities of sturgeon. Dapontes would have enjoyed this fish (possibly its caviar too) during his exile in Crimea in 1746–47. He was not the only one to appreciate its distinct flavor:

The Don [one of the rivers flowing into the Azov] . . .
is so abundant in fish, that in the year 1789, I bought
a waggon load of fish for the soldiers, for about three
shillings. Its Sturgeons and the fish called Sevruga, are
celebrated for their size and the delicacy of their flavour.
(Baron Campenhausen, *Travels through Several Provinces
of the Russian Empire . . .* , translator unknown, London:
Richard Phillips, 1808: 11)

seasoned beef of Kayseri   The city of Kayseri in central Anatolia
continues to be renowned for its *pastırma*. It was readily available
in the markets of Constantinople. See Ebru Boyar and Kate Fleet, *A
Social History of Ottoman Istanbul*, Cambridge: Cambridge University
Press, 2010): 152.

ODE IV

Indian diamonds . . . pearls   Precious stones were used in abundance
for imperial costumes, military ornaments, and the furnishing of the
sultan's palace. The following description, an eye-witness account by
a British visitor to the imperial treasury in 1840, gives a taste of what
Dapontes would have witnessed when he was invited in the imperial
palace in 1743 for the investiture of Ioannes Mavrokordatos:

> Here are thrones blazing with diamonds, rubies, pearls,
> and gold, including the celebrated throne of Nadir Shah,
> costumes of the sultan bedizened with sparkling jew-
> els, plumes with diamond fastenings, swords and dag-
> gers with hilts decorated with gems, shields elegantly
> wrought and jewelled, horse trappings, saddles and
> their coverings, embroidered with pearls and precious
> stones, knives, forks, spoons, and other articles of table
> service, clocks, inkstands, and snuff-boxes, all of them
> decorated in a similar manner. The imperial treasury
> holds a brilliant array of armor worn by the sultans; that

of Murad II., the conqueror of Bagdad, is mentioned
as being especially remarkable for its garniture of pre-
cious stones. . . . Costumes trimmed with valuable furs
and priceless gems, divans and cushions of gold tissue
wrought with pearls, cradles of solid gold inlaid with
precious stones, crystal vases encrusted with diamonds,
rubies, and emeralds, and numerous other articles,
equally rich in ornament, all afford proof of the former
wealth, power, and magnificence of the Turkish sultans.
(S. M. Burnham, *Precious Stones in Nature, Art, and Lit-
erature*, Boston: Bradlee Whidden, 1886: 66–67)

pearls from the Strait of Hormuz   The Strait of Hormuz connects
the Persian Gulf with that of Oman. The famous pearls of Hormuz,
extracted from the region for centuries, have been evoked as a symbol
of exotic riches by Milton in his description of Satan's seat:

High on a throne of royal state, which far
Outshone the wealth of Ormus and of Ind,
Or where the gorgeous East with richest hand
Showers on her kings barbaric pearl and gold.
(*Paradise Lost*, 2.1–4)

porcelain of China . . . and silk   Highly prized in the sultan's court
for use in table ware, ornaments, and mosque tiles, porcelain began
appearing in the material culture of the Ottoman Empire in the late
sixteenth century.

Venetian florins   A gold coin, also known as the *ducat*, it was used in
international trade together with the Dutch thaler and the Spanish
silver coin. One of the leading foreign coins to circulate in the empire,
it was used as a model for the *sultani* (Ottoman gold coin).

mammoth ivory of Moscow   Mammoth carcasses had been discov-
ered in Siberia since ancient times, their bones and tusks forming the

basis of the Moscow ivory trade that boomed in the sixteenth and seventeenth centuries.

corals of Sardinia   Red coral (*Corallium rubrum*) existed in large quantities in Sardinia, especially along the northwestern coast of Alghero. In Dapontes's time, the town of Torre del Greco in the province of Naples was the main port for Sardinia's coral fishing boats, becoming the world center for the production of red coral jewelry and cameos. Coral became a fashionable item in the Ottoman court in the eighteenth century, used to decorate weapons and horse trappings.

minerals of Trebizond   Located on the southern coast of the Black Sea at the crossroads of the empire's trade routes with India, Persia, and the Caucasus, the city of Trebizond held rich deposits of iron, silver, lead and copper; they contributed to the prosperity of the city, which became a flourishing center of Pontic Greek culture in the eighteenth century.

coffee from Yemen   By Dapontes's time, coffee was freely enjoyed in the Empire. This was not the case in earlier times, when the popularity of coffeehouses was perceived as a threat to the mosque, the traditional place of congregation. For the history of the legalization of coffee in the Ottoman Empire, see Ralph S. Hattox, *Coffee and Coffeehouses: The Origins of a Social Bevereage in the Medieval Near East*, Seattle: University of Washington Press, 1988.

cotton of Serres   The city of Serres in Macedonia, famous for its fabrics since the sixteenth century, was one of the main centers in the southern Balkans for the cultivation of cotton and the production of dyed cotton yarn, supplying both the Ottoman and the European markets and reaching its peak at the end of the eighteenth century. See Athanasios Gekas, "A Global History of Ottoman Cotton Textiles, 1600–1850," European University Institute Working Paper MWP 2007/30.

abundance of bees   An early-nineteenth-century geographer notes:

> Some boyars [of Wallachia] are known to possess six
> or even twelve thousand bee hives, which are usually
> formed in the hollow trunk of a tree. Before the division
> of the province, the prince derived a revenue of 60,000
> piastres from the tithe on honey and aromatic wax.
> (James Bell, *A System of Geography, Popular and Scientific*
> ..., Glasgow: Archibald Fullarton, 1832: 2:539)

stores of salt   On traveling north from Bucharest toward Focşani in
April 1758, Dapontes would have passed close to the town of Slănic,
whose salt lakes and mines had made the place famous as a center for
salt extraction.

Tripolitan soap   Dapontes is referring here to Tripoli in Lebanon,
which was then part of Ottoman Syria; not to be confused with the
capital of Libya or the city in the Peloponnese.

Latakia tobacco   Tobacco smoking had only recently become an
acceptable social practice, having raised a storm of religious and polit-
ical controversy when it was introduced a century earlier. Dapontes is
referring here to a special type of tobacco that derived its name from
Syria's port city, where it was produced. It was known in the empire as
"mountain tobacco"—a reference to its curing process, by which the
leaves were smoked over fragrant mountain herbs. It was one of the
most expensive and exclusive tobaccos available in the empire. See Relli
Shechter, "Tobacco in Early-Modern Ottoman Economy and Daily
Life," in *Smoking, Culture and Economy in the Middle East: The Egyptian
Tobacco Market, 1850–2000*, London: I. B. Tauris, 2006: 15–26.

the Tatars' arrows and bows   A reference to the Crimean Tatars who
were notorious for the frequent raids they conducted in southern
Russia and Ukraine. They had a reputation for being fearless fighters.

hazelnuts of Mount Athos   One of the few products exported from
the Holy Mountain in Dapontes's time. They are the subject of a

charming conversation purportedly held between the abbot of Karakallou Monastery and the British traveler Robert Curzon:

> All of a sudden, as we were walking quietly together, the agoumenos [abbot] asked me if I knew what was the price of nuts at Constantinople.
>
> "Nuts?" said I.
>
> "Yes, nuts," said he; "hazel-nuts: nuts are excellent things. Have they a good supply of nuts at Constantinople?"
>
> "Well," said I, "I don't know; but I dare say they have. But why, my Lord, do you ask? Why do you wish to know the price of hazel-nuts at Constantinople?"
>
> "Oh!" said the agoumenos, "they do not eat half nuts enough at Stamboul. Nuts are excellent things. They should be eaten more than they are. People say that nuts are unwholesome; but it is a great mistake." And so saying, he introduced me into a set of upper rooms that I had not previously entered, the entire floors of which were covered two feet deep with nuts. I never saw one-hundredth part so many before. The good agoumenos, it seems, had been speculating in hazel-nuts; and a vessel was to come to the little tower of the [S]caricatojo down below to be freighted with them: they were to produce a prodigious profit, and defray the expense of finishing the new buildings of Caracalla.
>
> "Take some," said he; "don't be afraid; there are plenty. Take some, and taste them, and then you can tell your friends at Constantinople what a peculiar flavour you found in the famous nuts of Athos; and in all Athos

every one knows that there are no nuts like those of Car-
acalla!" (Robert Curzon Jr., *Visits to Monasteries in the
Levant*, London: John Murray, 1849: 438–39)

Braşov   A city north of Bucharest and an important commercial
center along trade routes between the Ottoman Empire and the West.

Vlanga   A fertile area on the northern coast of Marmara (and now
known as Yenikapi), it used to serve as the capital's "garden district"
for the commercial cultivation of fruit and vegetables.

ODE V

icons of Moscow   The fourteenth century saw Moscow's rise as a
renowned center of Byzantine icon-painting; famous icon painters
such as Theophanes the Greek (ca. 1330–1410) and Andrei Rublev
(ca. 1370–1430) established a unique style that influenced the art
well into the seventeenth century. Dapontes was fortunate to be
presented with an icon from Moscow ("worth the whole of Wallachia
and Moldavia put together") during his appointment in the court of
Ioannes Mavrokordatos at Jassy (*Garden of Graces*, 3.379–96).

ladanum of Cyprus and Crete   An aromatic resin obtained from the
rockrose shrub.

kermes dye from the Peloponnese   A crimson dye obtained from the
crushed bodies of the insect *Kermes vermilio*, a parasite on the kermes
oak, which is native to the Mediterranean. The dye was used exten-
sively in the production of Ottoman carpets and robes.

Moscow's furs   One of the chief items that Greek merchants
imported to Constantinople from Moscow, center of the fur trade
since the seventeenth century. A mark of status and wealth, furs
were in high demand among the Ottoman elite, not least by the
sultan himself, who wore a different fur robe on each occasion
and whose seasonal change of robe was marked by an elaborate
ceremony. The importance of furs as a symbol of rank and political

office in the Ottoman administration was seen at the investiture of Prince Ioannes Mavrokordatos, which Dapontes witnessed himself. See above, pp. 4–7.

Basra's sweet sultans   The *Centaurea imperialis*, a plant with fragrant pink flowers, native to the Middle East.

Mani quails   A large number of quails were caught in the Mani peninsula, especially in the bay of Porto Kagio on the southern tip of the peninsula. The name of the bay is a corruption of "Porto Quaglio," given by the Venetians after the large flocks of quails caught there during the birds' annual migration to Italy.

Euboean sucuk   Euboea was Dapontes's last stop on his mission before sailing back to Mount Athos in 1765. There he may have tasted this local delicacy, a sausage-shaped confection made with walnuts and must.

honey from Athens   Felix Beaujour, who served as the French consul in Thessalonike and was a contemporary of Dapontes, notes:

> The Athenian honey . . . bears so high a value, that it constitutes, on that account, an article of luxury in the commerce of Greece. This article is exported almost wholly to Constantinople, where it is consumed in the imperial palace, and in the seraglios of the great. Of all the European cities, London and Marseilles are the only ones that receive some trifling quantities, which the merchants of those two places distribute, by way of presents, to their friends. (*A View of the Commerce of Greece, Formed after an Annual Average, from 1787 to 1797*, trans. Thomas Hartwell Horne, London: James Wallis, 1800: 114)

Venetian piacentino   Probably a reference to grana piacentino, a hard, dry cheese produced in the city of Piacenza near Venice and exported to Constantinople.

Little tunny of Chios . . . mackerel from the Sea of Marmara The fish mentioned in these troparia reflect the variety that was available in Constantinople's vibrant fish market, an attraction for foreign visitors to the city:

> The narrow alleys leading from the two landing-places called Balyk-Bazar 'Skellessy, terminate in a broader street, running parallel to the city walls. This is the fish market, where the display is more remarkable for abundance and variety than for size or quality. The divers species are exposed on leaden or wooden dressers, the finer kinds suspended by the gills, the smaller in large wooden bowls. Shell fish, when in season, especially muscles, are kept in baskets, and are brought to market in boundless profusion.
>
> The balykjee's (fishmongers) shops offer none of the neatness that generally characterizes those of Europe. . . .
>
> The abundance of sea fish is remarkable, and the varieties of the smaller kinds numerous. Providence, in its great bounty, has been more liberal in this respect to the Bosphorus than to any other waters in Europe. Many species are unknown to our markets, and some are complete strangers to our seas. The extraordinary beauty of colours observed in some varieties is highly interesting; green, gold, pink, azure, red, and silver, glisten in brilliant tints upon their scales. (Charles White, *Three Years in Constantinople; or, Domestic Manners of the Turks in 1844*, London: Henry Colburn, 1845: 1.73–74)

The same account makes reference to the "extraordinary size" of Smyrna's prawns. Legendary even in antiquity (Athenaeus, *The Deipnosophistis*, 1.12), they did not fail impress other contemporary travelers too; Marianne Young, for example, would exclaim: "monstrous—quite curiosities are the giant prawns of Smyrna" (*Our Camp in Turkey, and the Way to It*, London: Richard Bentley, 1854: 137). Equally impressive in size were the eels of Ioannina: "The lake of Ioannina abounds in fish, of which the eels are remarkable for the great size they attain" (Henry Holland, *Travels in the Ionian Isles . . .*, London, 1815: 140). Dapontes was very fond of fish. In a personal letter written during his imprisonment he recalls "those well-cooked, succulent fish / filled with a thousand spices and herbs" ("Τὰ ψάρια τὰ καλόβραστα καὶ τὰ καλοζουμάτα, / μὲ χίλια ἡδύσματα, μυρωδικὰ γεμάτα" [Kechagioglou 1986: 43]).

Koutali   Today, Ekinlik; one of the smaller islands in the Sea of Marmara.

Constantinople's oysters   Celebrated also by Alexander Pushkin in "Onegin's Travels":

We careless fellows leave the fretting
To merchants; we have but one fear:
The load of oysters they were getting
From Istamboul may not be here.
The oysters? They have come! In rapture
Forth rushes greedy youth to capture
Those fleshy anchorites alive
And gulp them down as they arrive,
Just for a dash of lemon waiting.
(*Eugene Onegin: A Novel in Verse*, trans. Babette Deutsch, ed.
Avrahm Yarmolinsky [New York: Heritage Press, 1943], 162–63)

Tuzla   A small fishing town located on the coast of the Sea of Marmara, east of Constantinople and close to the island of Halki, where Dapontes had stayed for a brief period in 1748.

ODE VI

The plane tree in Vostitsa and Kos   Two famous trees: the first, an enormous plane tree on the beach in the town of Vostitsa (modern-day Aigio) on the northern coast of the Peloponnese, famous for being next to a fountain described by Pausanias (*Description of Greece*, 7.24.3); the second, the legendary "tree of Hippocrates," located in the main town of the island of Kos, birthplace of the ancient physician, who is said to have taught his pupils under the shade of this tree.

olive groves on Thasian shores   Setting off from Mount Athos in May 1757, Dapontes sailed past the island of Thasos; he was impressed by the rows of olive trees lining its coast (*Garden of Graces*, 6.21–24).

Paris's palace and parks   Appointed ambassador to France in 1720, the Ottoman statesman Yirmisekiz Mehmed Çelebi Efendi wrote an account of French culture and customs, including a detailed description of the Tuileries Palace gardens, which Dapontes is probably referring to here. Dapontes included a Greek translation of this work ("Περιγραφὴ τῆς Φράντζας ...") in his unpublished "Geographical History." Parts of his translation appear in Legrand 1880–88, 3:lxii–lxiv.

peaks of Athos and Olympus   In a footnote to this line, Dapontes notes that the peaks of Olympus are two. The second is Mount Olympus of ancient Mysia (now known as Mount Uludağ, near Bursa); like Mount Athos, this was a monastic center in Byzantine times (see also *Garden of Graces*, 16.241–42).

Bizye   The ancient name of modern-day Vize, a town in the province of Kırklareli in the Marmara region of Turkey; it is renowned for its natural beauty and resources. Dapontes may well have been there in person as it was close to both Adrianople and Constantinople. It also featured an early Byzantine cave monastery of the sort that fascinated Dapontes.

ODE VII

my Lady's girdle and gown   According to Dapontes, these relics were kept in the Vatopedi Monastery on Mount Athos (*Garden of Graces*, 16.83–84).

the relics of Saint Spyridon   The relics of the patron saint of Corfu.

Vlatadon   The fourteenth-century monastery in Thessalonike, named Tsaous Monastery during Ottoman rule, after the Turkish governor of the city. It underwent a full restoration in the latter half of the eighteenth century.

that of Luke in Steiri of Phocis   One of the largest to survive from the Middle Byzantine period, the Monastery of Hosios Loukas in Boeotia is renowned worldwide for its unique architecture, lavish murals, and mosaics.

the hundred-gate church on the island of Paros   Early Byzantine church complex in the port town of Parikia; parts of it date from the fourth century. It is famous for its size, elaborate architecture, and ancient baptismal font.

Sarindar Monastery   A monastery in Bucharest. See also *Garden of Graces*, 4.235ff., 6.67–68.

Great Cave Monastery in the Peloponnese   Built into the rock of Mount Helmos in the northern region of the Peloponnese, near Kalavryta.

ODE VIII

Kiev Cave Monastery   Founded by the hermit St. Anthony in the early eleventh century, it was initially a small underground cave, developing over the centuries into a large subterranean complex that contained several chapels and the tombs and relics of many notables and saints. The bell tower, consisting of three colonnaded levels and a gilt dome, was a monumental addition to the monastery and a recent construction in Dapontes's time, completed only in 1745.

bell tower in Saint Petersburg   The 120-meter bell tower of the cathedral of Saints Peter and Paul was another "modern" construction, topped by an impressive copper gilt spire. It was completed in 1733.

Saint Peter's in Rome   See also *Garden of Graces*, 16.145–46.

Holy Trinity of Pechersk   The twelfth-century Church of the Holy Trinity in the entrance way to the Kiev Cave Monastery, mentioned above.

church in Saint Petersburg . . . Saint Luke   A reference to the eighteenth-century church in the Smolensk Cemetery in St. Petersburg. It was dedicated to the famous "Smolensk icon" of the Mother of God, attributed to St. Luke. Numerous churches in Russia were dedicated to this famous icon, housing copies of the original. Dapontes's aside ("as they say") suggests that he was aware that the icon of the Mother of God in the said church in St. Petersburg was not the original one.

church with the tombs of the Tsars   The cathedral of Saints Peter and Paul in St. Petersburg, containing the tombs of the emperors and empresses of Russia from Peter the Great.

tomb of Muhammad   Housed in the Al-Masjid al-Nabawi, the Prophet's mosque in the city of Medina, now one of the world's largest mosques.

peninsulas of Cyzicus   The ancient site of Cyzicus is found on a triangular piece of land projecting out into the Sea of Marmara from the northern coast of Anatolia; it is now known as the Kapu-dagh peninsula.

bridge across Euripus to get across to Europe   Since antiquity, several bridges had been built across the Euripus Strait to connect the island of Euboea to the mainland. Dapontes might seem to be exaggerating when he says that the bridge across Euripus connected one to Europe (a remark he repeats in the *Garden of Graces*, 14.83–88), but Euboea was indeed the only island in the Aegean with a bridge connecting it to the mainland, whereby one was then connected to the continent. Dapontes would have crossed this bridge during his one-month stay on Euboea in September 1765, the last recorded stop on his mission before his return to Mount Athos. A description of the bridge in the early nineteenth century by John Cam Hobhouse, Lord Byron's traveling companion, affords a glimpse of what it must have looked like in Dapontes's time:

> We dismounted, and led our horses over a narrow wooden bridge, about fifteen paces in length, to a stone tower in the middle of the [Euripus] strait, of an odd circular shape, like a dice-box, large at bottom and top, and small in the middle; the mouths of immense cannon appearing through round embrasures, about the upper rim. Going through an arch in this tower, we passed on to a bridge, also of wood, and a third longer than the other, standing over the principal stream, for such may the Euripus strictly be called. (*A Journey through Albania, and Other Provinces of Turkey in Europe and Asia, to Constantinople, during the Years 1809 and 1810* [Philadelphia: M. Carey and Son, 1817], 1:365–66)

Bursa's baths   These sulphur-rich thermal baths were renowned since antiquity for their therapeutic properties, acquired a cult-like status under the Ottomans, possibly following the springs' former significance as a sacred Christian site.

porcelain tower of China   The nine-tiered, 80-meter-high porcelain pagoda in Nanjing, constructed in the fifteenth century, was a widely admired example of Chinese architecture; it contributed to the European and Ottoman fascination with oriental culture in the seventeenth and eighteenth centuries.

torazzo of Cremona   The 112-meter-high bell tower of the Cathedral of Cremona in northern Italy, built in the early fourteenth century. Dapontes's list of marvels echoes here the popular adage: "Unus Petrus est in Roma, / Una turris in Cremona, / Unus portus in Ancona."

bridges of China, Venice, and Adrianople, as well as those of Çekmece   Dapontes would have known about China's bridges from Georgios Fatseas's translation of *Geography Anatomiz'd* by Patrick Gordon (Γραμματικὴ γεωγραφικὴ ... [Venice: Antonio Zatta, 1760], 2:315–16). The bridges of Adrianople and Çekmece (a western suburb in Constantinople) he visited in person (*Garden of Graces*, 6.31–35, 16.399–400). Many of those in Adrianople were designed by the renowned imperial architect and engineer Mimar Sinan, whose mosques, palaces and other public buildings (including the famous arch bridge in Çekmece) are considered masterpieces of Ottoman architecture.

tides of Tigris, Euripus and Euphrates   See also *Garden of Graces*, 14.89–100.

sea of Amsterdam   A reference either to the Zuiderzee (which in Dapontes's time was still an inlet of the North Sea in the north-western part of Holland, extending south as far as Amsterdam) or to canal rings constructed in Amsterdam in the seventeenth century.

Kinburn cape   During his exile in Crimea, Dapontes may have visited this impressive promontory, a long narrow strip of land in the Black Sea, extending westward from Kherson.

Lake Moeris   An artificial lake, once covering the whole Fayum basin in Egypt. See also *Garden of Graces*, 16.157–58.

ODE IX

Our faith . . . and Indian simplicity   These two troparia reflect the religious, cultural, and ethnic diversity that characterized Dapontes's world in the eighteenth century. On this subject, see Benjamin Braude and Bernard Lewis, eds., *Christians and Jews in the Ottoman Empire: The Functioning of a Plural Society*, 2 vols. (New York: Holmes & Meier, 1982); and Donald Quataert, *The Ottoman Empire, 1700–1922*, 2nd ed. (Cambridge: Cambridge University Press, 2005), 174–94. Dapontes includes groups with a shared faith in Orthodoxy ("Russian reverence"), as well as groups involved in contemporary political and military events: the reference to the "Prussian army" is most likely associated with the emergence of Prussia as a major European power at the end of the Seven Years' War (1756–63); "Iberian liberty," a reference to the repulse of the Spanish invasion of Portugal in 1762 in the context of the same war (see also *Garden of Graces*, 16.1249–50). The "current war" most likely refers to the Russo-Turkish war (1768–74) that had ended with a decisive Russian victory, four years before the publication of the "Canon of Hymns."

zeal of Elijah . . . and Samson's valor and strength   Dapontes describes these Old Testament figures in detail in the *Mirror of Women* (1:6–23, 383–93; and 2:49–126, 332–35).

wonders of the world   In addition to the traditional seven wonders of the ancient world (mentioned also in the *Garden of Graces*, 16.401–14), Dapontes includes here two more: the Egyptian labyrinth (see also *Garden of Graces*, 16.161–64), originally described by Herodotus; and the theatre of Heraclea, which was often included in lists of ancient wonders compiled by medieval Latin authors, such as Gregory of Tours and the Venerable Bede. According to Bede ("De Septem Mundi Miraculis"), the Theatre of Heraclea was

> carved out of one piece of marble, so that all the cells and rooms of the wall, and the dens of the beasts, are

made out of one solid stone. It is supported on four
arches carved out of the same stone; and no one can
whisper in the whole circle so low, either to himself or to
another, without being heard by every one who is in the
circle of the building. (*The Biographical Writings and Let-
ters of Venerable Bede*, trans. J. A. Giles [London: James
Bohn, 1845], 157–58)

Notice

an unscrupulous copyist or copy editor   The person in question is
Thomas Mandakasis, a doctor from Kastoria who provided finan-
cial support to the Greek printing press in Leipzig. Further details
regarding Dapontes's grievances against Mandakasis for mishandling
the *Mirror of Women* can be found in Savvidis 1993: 182–87.

deformed my work   The same grievance had been expressed earlier
in "Βίβλος βασιλειῶν":

A book may take over a year to compose
With such diligence, labor and pain.
A copyist showing no respect or remorse
Will then ruin it in a month or a week.

Dapontes goes on to compare his deformed book to a "pitiful
monster" with fingers on its feet instead of toes (Savvidis 1991a:
42–44).

Letters on Pride and the Vanity of Human Life

On the Vanity of the World and the Woes of Man

a wisp of smoke   Cf. James 4:14: "What is your life? For you are a
mist that appears for a little while and then vanishes."

All is vanity   Dapontes was clearly influenced by *Ecclesiastes*; these lines are the strongest echo of the Old Testament text on the futility and transience of human life.

Alexander the Great . . . chanced upon Diogenes   A rather loose version of the famous anecdote, originally recorded by Plutarch, concerning the meeting of Alexander the Great with Diogenes the Cynic: the famed ruler visited the philosopher in Corinth, expecting to receive the usual flattery and praise. However, Diogenes, who was lying on the ground, only asked Alexander to "stand a little out of [his] sun"— leaving the general deeply impressed by the philosopher's disregard for power and fame ("Alexander," in *Lives*, trans. Bernadotte Perrin, vol. 7, Loeb Classical Library [Cambridge, MA: Harvard University Press, 1919], 14.1–5).

the prince and his principality   Dapontes's personal contact with the princes in the courts at Bucharest and Jassy gave him direct insight into their extravagant lifestyle, of which he is critical here. His criticism was shared by many, most notably by Mark Philip Zallony in his scathing essay on the Phanariots (Zallony 1826).

Index

〜

Bucharest. See Wallachia
Bursa, 104, 105, 118, 121

Chios, xxx, xxxi, 103
Constantinople, xviii, xix, xln79, li,
    97-122 passim. See also under
    Dapontes, Konstantinos
Crimea. See under Dapontes,
    Konstantinos

Dapontes, Konstantinos: alms-
    collecting mission, xvii, xxix-
    xxxii, xlvii, xlviiin103, 101,
    103, 107, 108, 112, 115, 118,
    121; in Constantinople, xx,
    xxii, xxiii, xxv, xxvii-xxviii, xxx,
    xxxi, 106, 122; critical recep-
    tion, xiv-xviii passim, xxviiin38,
    xxxix, l; education, xvii-xix;
    influenced by Enlightenment,
    xviii-xix, xxxiii, xxxvi-xli, exile
    in Crimea, xxiii-xxiv, xxxi,
    xlii-xliii, xliv, xlvii, 108, 122;
    on Halki, xxvii, 117; imprison-
    ment, xxv, xxvii, xxxi, xlii, 117;
    Kaisarios, change of name

to, xxviii; marriage, xxvii; in
    Moldavia, xix, xxii-xxiv, xxv,
    xxxi, xlviiin103, 97, 101, 102,
    103, 114-115, 125; Monastery
    of Evangelistria (Skopelos), xvii-
    xviii, xxiv, xxxivn57; monastic
    vows. See Piperi; mother, xxvii;
    on Mount Athos, xxix-xxx,
    xxxiv-xxxv, xxxvin60, xxxviii;
    outcast, xiii, xx-xxi, xxiii-xxv,
    xxviii, xxxi, xlii-xliii, l-li; contact
    with Phanariots, xv, xviii-xxiii,
    xxix-xxx, xlii, xlv, li, lii, 102, 125;
    on Piperi, xxviii-xxix, xxxi, xliii,
    xlix, li; on Skopelos, xv, xvii-xix,
    xx, xxiin19, xxix, xxx, xxxiv, xlvii,
    102; spirituality, xiv, xxiv-xxv,
    xxxiii, xli-xlv, xlix-lii passim.
    See also Piperi; Hesychasm;
    travels, xxx-xxxiv. See also alms-
    collecting mission; in Wallachia,
    xviii-xxi, xxv, xxix, xxviin36,
    xlii, 97, 102, 125; writings,
    subjectivity in, xiv, xv, xxv-xxvi,
    xxxiv, xliii-xlvi; zeteia. See alms-
    collecting mission

127